Service User Involvement

of related interest

Co-Production and Personalization in Social Care
Changing Relationships in the Provision of Social Care
Edited by Susan Hunter and Pete Ritchie
Research Highlights in Social Work Series
ISBN 978 1 84310 558 9

Developments in Social Work with Offenders
Edited by Gill McIvor and Peter Raynor
Research Highlights in Social Work Series
ISBN 978 1 84310 538 1

Competence in Social Work Practice
A Practical Guide for Students and Professionals
Second Edition
Edited by Kieran O'Hagan
ISBN 978 1 84310 485 8

Supporting Women after Domestic Violence
Loss, Trauma and Recovery
Hilary Abrahams
Foreword by Cathy Humphreys
ISBN 978 1 84310 431 5

Morals, Rights and Practice in the Human Services
Marie Connolly and Tony Ward
ISBN 978 1 84310 486 5

'Race', Housing and Social Exclusion
Edited by Peter Somerville and Andy Steele
ISBN 978 1 85302 849 6

Community Care Practice and the Law
3rd Edition
Michael Mandelstam
ISBN 978 1 84310 233 5

Homeless Children
Problems and Needs
Edited by Panos Vostanis and Stuart Cumella
ISBN 978 1 85302 595 2

Fostering Now
Messages from Research
Ian Sinclair
*Foreword by Tom Jeffreys, Director General, Children, Families
and Young People Directorate, DfES*
ISBN 978 1 84310 362 2

Service User Involvement
Reaching the Hard to Reach
in Supported Housing

Helen Brafield and Terry Eckersley

Jessica Kingsley Publishers
London and Philadelphia

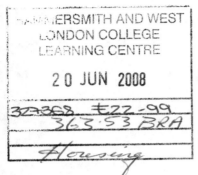
First published in 2008
by Jessica Kingsley Publishers
116 Pentonville Road
London N1 9JB, UK
and
400 Market Street, Suite 400
Philadelphia, PA 19106, USA

www.jkp.com

Library of Congress Cataloging in Publication Data

Brafield, Helen, 1956-
  Service user involvement : reaching the hard to reach in supported housing / Helen Brafield and Terry Eckersley.
    p. cm.
  Includes bibliographical references and index.
  ISBN 978-1-84310-343-1 (alk. paper)
  1. People with social disabilities--Services for--Great Britain. 2. People with social disabilities--Housing--Great Britain. 3. Social service--Great Britain--Citizen participation. 4. Housing policy--Great Britain--Citizen participation. 5. Counselor and client--Great Britain. I. Eckersley, Terry, 1961- II. Title.
  HV245.B74 2007
  362.4'0480941--dc22
                                          2007028350

British Library Cataloguing in Publication Data
A CIP catalogue record for this book is available from the British Library

ISBN 978 1 84310 343 1

Printed and bound in Great Britain by
Athenaeum Press, Gateshead, Tyne and Wear

322368

Contents

Preface

GUIDE TO SERVICE USER INVOLVEMENT

This book came about thanks to Terry Eckersley's enthusiasm that 'we should write a book' and because I thought it made sense to offer a practical guide to a topic that professionals in the supported housing field are still struggling with. In April 2003 the then Office of the Deputy Prime Minister (ODPM) set up the Supporting People programme, a new regime for funding supported housing. A fundamental tenet was proposed that service users should be at the centre of service planning and delivery, and some service providers just didn't think they knew how to do it.

We are not saying there is no good practice in this area. Clearly there is, but we don't know about all of it, so don't be offended if you already do good stuff! It seems to be a feature of the voluntary sector that good practice is not publicised, probably because people just don't have time to do it and advertise it!

We are particularly interested in effectively consulting with people who historically have been marginalised by society and are not used to anyone asking for, listening to, or acting on their views. These people often have greater and more immediate priorities than taking part in consultation processes – such as finding food and shelter.

ROCC (originally the Resettlement of Offenders Coordinating Committee) is a registered charity based in Hampshire, providing support, consultancy and training to its member organisations. In turn, these organisations provide housing-related support services to vulnerable people. In 2002, the then Director of ROCC, Beth Taylor, secured a large grant from the then ODPM, John Prescott, to conduct an action research project on how to consult with 'hard-to-reach' service users for strategic planning under this new government initiative 'Supporting People'.

As a result of my work in this sector, for charities and as an independent consultant and trainer, I was fortunate enough to get a contract with ROCC for this project, with an emphasis on involvement at the strategic level.

The Supporting People programme pooled all the previous financial sources into one and aimed to put the service user at the centre of the support they received. The programme made a clearer distinction between rent, care, and support, and the 'support' element had to demonstrate that it was directly related to enabling individuals to live as independently as possible in their accommodation.

Having then worked for over 15 years in supported housing services, mostly for homeless people fulfilling the hard-to-reach criteria, I was very keen to get involved. I was appointed project manager and supported by a team of approved consultants. The role of the consultants was to consult with service users deemed particularly hard to reach, as well as commissioners of housing-related support services now working under the Supporting People programme. The work was complex and difficult, as we were looking at a number of issues and at a number of different levels. We wanted to answer the following questions:

- Who are hard-to-reach service users?
- If they are hard to reach, how will we engage with them?
- What is consultation?
- How are users' views currently collected and applied at the basic level of service delivery?
- Should we consult service users about the highest level (strategic planning), and if so, how?

The findings were interesting and varied and we have used them to underpin the book where appropriate. Overall, we were able to establish some do's and don'ts for consulting with hard-to-reach service users and there was an emphasis on more creative methods than 'sitting in boring meetings'.

We proposed a model of service user involvement and this contributed to the shape of the final models, proposed for consultation at the strategic level, which have since been adopted by at least two local authorities.

I was asked to present the research and findings at the ROCC Annual General Meeting in October 2003, and was approached afterwards by the housing manager of the Southampton YMCA, Terry Eckersley. He said he had found it very interesting, that he too had a passion for user involvement, and that we should write a book together!

I did not take this suggestion too seriously at the time, but over the year 2004–05 interest in the findings had generated sufficiently for ROCC to be asked to deliver training on how to consult effectively with hard-to-reach service users, as well as present the findings at various events and conferences.

In addition, ROCC was asked to set up and run groups for service users to inform strategic planning at the highest level for two local authorities, Hampshire and Portsmouth. Both of these Service User Reference Groups are now underway, and ROCC and I are still being asked for advice and help in this area, so I decided that perhaps it was a good idea to produce a practical workbook for all staff and managers providing or commissioning housing-related support services to better develop the involvement of their service users.

This book therefore uses findings of the initial research, subsequent development, and examples of current good practice to provide a clear guide to effective consultation with hard-to-reach service users at all levels, with, for the first time that we are aware of, a focus on the strategic level.

We really hope that people find this book useful as a practical guide for consulting with service users in any service and at any level.

We believe that the not-for-profit sector tends to suffer from a lack of self-promotion. We should all be exchanging our good ideas for the benefit of everybody!

Please let us hear about any good practice examples you would like to share.

Helen Brafield

Acknowledgements

HELEN BRAFIELD

I would like to thank the former Office of the Deputy Prime Minister for funding the initial ROCC (originally Resettlement of Offenders Coordinating Committee) research into consulting with hard-to-reach service users for strategic planning, and Beth Taylor for giving me the opportunity to do it.

I would like to thank Simon Mantle, Nicky Youern (Chair) and Nichola Goom (Chief Executive) of ROCC for giving their consent to my using the final report that I wrote for the ROCC research as the basis of this book.

I would like to thank ROCC associate consultants who contributed to the ROCC research: Derek Adams, Ian Barrett, Irene MacWilliam and Marc Mordey.

I would like to thank Alan Hagger and Graham Woods from Hampshire Supporting People for funding and contributing to the first Hampshire Service User Reference Group.

I would also like to thank all those professionals and volunteers who are committed to service user consultation, and in particular those who took the time to contribute their good practice examples or case studies for the book.

I would also like to thank the service users who have inspired me to keep on promoting their value and abilities to be consulted with at the highest levels, and in turn involve others, especially those on the Hampshire and Portsmouth Service User Reference Groups, and particularly those who have made direct contributions to the book: Kelly Spencer, Douglas Mallett and James Lovelock.

TERRY ECKERSLEY

I would like to thank Keith Wells, former Chief Executive Officer of Sheffield YMCA, for epitomising service user involvement, and current CEO David Reynolds and Company Secretary Neville Chambers for keeping that dream alive. Thanks too to Tony Frowd, Chief Executive at Southampton YMCA, for his patience and support.

I would also like to thank my former pastors, David Gilpin and Pastor Andrew Elmes, who don't just teach empowerment but live and breathe it.

Appreciation to my current pastor, Gary Clarke, for encouraging us to dream big.

Many thanks too to the housing management team at Southampton YMCA for all their hard work, diligence and loyalty and for continuing to involve the service users with excellence, compassion and creativity. Also to the board who employed me to set up Woking YMCA, and to the staff, volunteers and partners who are making service user involvement a reality.

Our warmest thanks also go to all the service users who contributed anonymously to the project, plus professionals and commissioners: Alan Hagger, Andrea Ribbons, Andrew Palmer, Ann Woolnough, Audrey Hollingbury, Beth Taylor, Bonnie, Brian Sheath, Brian Taylor, Carol Kavanagh, Carol Lean, Carole Binns, Cecilia Adjabe, Claire Mynott, Clive Coldwell, Dawn Buck, Derek Adams, Don John, Don Moat, Dr Ian Barrett, Elaine Barnes, Emily, George Summers, Graham Woods, Gregory Roberts, Ian Caren, Irene MacWilliam, Jane Abraham, Jo Dare, Lois Brewster, Lyn Watson, Marc Mordey, Martin Pearl, Mary Lloyd, Maureen Calloway, Micky Richards, Mohammed Mossadaq, Morag Currie, Paul Davies, Richard Chorley, Sharon, Sharon Picken, Simon Mantle, Stuart Hayes, Wayne, Winchester College, and Yvonne May.

Notes on the text:

The former Office of the Deputy Prime Minister is currently called Communities and Local Government.

Please note that any mention of governmental departments have not taken into consideration the changes that took place to them in June 2007.

Some service users' names have been changed to protect their identity.

Introduction

WELCOME

We know that those of you in the social care and voluntary sector want the most for your clients or service users. We also know that you are always pushed for time and money. At the centre of your practice, however, should be the core value of empowerment for individuals to make the best of themselves. Because you may be too busy to spend a lot of time reading books, we have put together a practical guide to involving service users in the care and support they receive. At the end of each chapter there are questions or exercises to do that follow a simple but structured framework. For those of you keen to learn more there are the chapters of useful information, and case studies demonstrating good practice that we have come across in the field but which is rarely publicised.

WHO SHOULD READ THIS BOOK?

This book provides useful information, interesting case studies, and above all a practical guide for anyone working to provide a service for vulnerable people in the not-for-profit sector, whether they are funders, providers, staff, or service users. You may be working in supported housing, or day services, and with any or all client groups, but we hope that you can make use of the ideas here to fit your specific circumstances.

WHAT IS THE PURPOSE OF THIS BOOK?

The purpose of the book is to provide you with relevant background material, so that you can use some or all of it to develop or strengthen your service user consultation and involvement within your organisation. This may be one small service, a large complex charity, or a funding body wanting to consult with a variety of service users to enable their strategic planning.

In addition, this book provides very practical guidance to help you and your organisation develop and produce an effective and workable strategy for consulting service users, covering all aspects from policy and procedures to the culture change needed to embed such practices. It also contains examples of good practice in the field, as well as case studies presented in more depth, that the authors have come across in the course of their research. This selection is in no way exhaustive, but can certainly give you ideas for your own work.

WHAT IS MEANT BY 'SERVICE USERS'?

Throughout the book, one of the authors have used the term 'service users' to mean any of the following groups who use housing-related support services: participants, tenants, residents, citizens, clients or 'people'. The usage depends on the circumstances and the point being made. Service users the authors met did not like the description 'service user' but so far no-one has identified a generic term that makes a useful distinction, where one needs to be made for clarity. In the book, the term 'service user' holds no value judgement, but if we called everyone 'people' it would be hard to know *which* people we were talking about!

Many service users would also object to the term 'vulnerable' but the authors have included it where necessary to make a distinction and because that is the reason used by the Supporting People programme for funding services. It could be that an individual's circumstances have put them in a vulnerable position, or they may be vulnerable to abuse from others, or vulnerable to addictions. The idea of Supporting People is, however, to empower individuals to live as full and independent a life as possible so that over time and within their own circumstances they will be less vulnerable.

WHAT IS SUPPORTING PEOPLE?

This government initiative went live in 2005. The principal ideas were to streamline the funding that supported housing services received, make a distinction between payments for rent and support, and make providers of such services more accountable via a variety of qualitative and quantitative measures. A core tenet was that of users being central to the service that they received, so that they were empowered to develop to the best of their abilities and live as independently as possible.

ABOUT THIS BOOK

Each chapter in this book focuses on a particular area of relevance to effective service user consultation. You can read the chapters in any order: you may prefer to dip in and out of them as you see fit, depending on your interest and the needs of your organisation.

At the end of Chapters 1, 3, 4, 5, 6 and 8 you will find a practical workbook section including questions and activities that, when followed through, can help you create a strategy for comprehensive service user involvement at all levels of your organisation. Chapter 2 outlines the authors' experience of an action research project. Chapter 8 is devoted to helping you develop your strategy, which should be straightforward if you have completed the workbooks in the previous chapters.

The questions and activities can be completed by an individual or team in any organisation offering services to vulnerable people. The authors strongly recommend making full use of these tools, as they will help you replicate, refine and adapt the other material for your own particular service users.

GOOD PRACTICE

Throughout the book we provide some excellent examples of how to set up innovative and practical projects. We have selected these examples because they either

- focus on hard-to-reach groups or could be adapted for other groups

or

- demonstrate commitment to consultation with service users
- describe how to overcome potential barriers, use good communication or other creative consultative methods, etc.
- can be used for consultation at any level, including strategic planning.

In the course of our research we examined many case studies, which have been presented in detail. This selection is by no means exhaustive but can give you ideas for your own work.

Here is a list of the case studies, organised by chapter.

Chapter 3: Barriers and Enablers to Effective Service User Consultation

- *Case study 3.1* Atlantic Housing Ltd: star code system for commitment
- *Case study 3.2* Worthing Churches Homeless Projects (WCHP) and service user involvement
- *Case study 3.3* Richard's story.

Chapter 4: Methods that Enable Client Consultation

- *Case study 4.1* Southampton BME Housing Project

SOME USEFUL DEFINITIONS

Before embarking on a substantial strategy of service user consultation or involvement it is worth spending a little time reflecting to what degree you and your organisation wish to consult with, or involve, service users. These terms are often used interchangeably but are worth unpicking so that everyone knows what it is you are collectively trying to do.

In *Service User Participation and Homelessness Services: Concepts, Trends, Practices* (Velasco 2001), the author lists 11 terms in common usage. These terms relate to the degrees to which service users are engaged in participation, involvement and consultation. Here is a shorter and perhaps more user-friendly list: service user involvement, user participation, user consultation, user empowerment, acting together, deciding together (as produced by the Community Care Needs Assessment Project (CCNAP 2001) website, www.ccnap.org.uk).

Terms and abbreviations

It might be helpful here to state the authors' policy in dealing with abbreviations. Where terms are used continuously throughout the book, the full wording is provided the first time they are used in each chapter, and thereafter the abbreviation is used.

AA Alcoholics Anonymous

acting together working with others to make decisions and carry through the action agreed. This may be appropriate when:
- there is a shared agenda
- there is an ongoing process of development of trust and cooperation between the parties
- the imbalance of power or resources has been addressed.

Best Value review An auditing tool used to assess best value/quality for money in the public sector, by assessing costs, quality, and stakeholder feedback of one agency with other similar organisations

BME Black and Minority Ethnic, origin of individuals or groups

CCG County Core Group, the highest decision-making body in each region for the Supporting People programme in the UK

CCNAP Community Care Needs Assessment Project

CDAT Community Drug Action Team

CVS Council for Voluntary Services

service user involvement a generic term that could be used to describe almost any activity or initiative

DAAT Drug and Alcohol Action Team

DTLR The Department of Transport, Local Government and Regions

deciding together This is where a group shares views, jointly generates options and decides upon a course of action. Deciding together is appropriate when:
- there is a possibility of negotiation
- an agreed agenda needs to be reached among different interests
- implementation requires the cooperation of other people.

GLO Gypsy Liaison Officer, local authority employee with this responsibility

IT information technology

MORI Market and Opinion Research International – provides independent polls of population's opinions

NTA National Treatment Agency

ODPM Formerly Office of the Deputy Prime Minister

PCT Primary Care Trust – local regional health bodies

QAF Quality Assurance Framework – self-assessment tool for providers of housing-related support services developed by the Supporting People programme. Higher grades are commensurate with higher degrees of service user consultation and involvement in the service.

ROCC (originally Resettlement of Offenders Coordinating Committee) is a registered charity based in Hampshire, providing support, consultancy and training to its member organisations. In turn, these organisations provide housing-related support services to vulnerable people.

Supporting People – UK Government agenda for funding housing-related support services for vulnerable people

SURG Service User Reference Group – a new group set up to feed service users' views to the core group

user consultation The gathering of information and/or opinions from users about existing services or plans for changes or new services drawn up by the organisation. This can also be defined as market research. Consultation can also be defined as allowing choice between limited, pre-determined options, but not an opportunity to propose alternatives or take part in putting plans into action. Consultation (only) may then be appropriate when the range of options is genuinely limited.

user empowerment this is a process through which users are empowered to influence decisions about their own individual circumstances and/or services and organisations. Empowerment can be initiated either by users themselves, or by workers, managers and governors/trustees in organisations. In addition, service user consultation can be taken to involve service users by making decisions and acting in partnership.

user participation a generic term, although narrower than 'service user involvement', suggesting that users are taking a part in some aspect of the organisation's work and therefore have some influence in decision-making.

YMCA Young Men's Christian Association, well-established international charity supporting vulnerable people.

CHAPTER 1

Models of Service User Participation

INTRODUCTION

Models of service user participation are many and varied, and, although interesting in themselves as a way of understanding the values and dynamics of the processes, they also have practical applications for planning and evaluating participation initiatives.

A good place to start is by looking at how much control service users are to be given – that is, what sort of decisions will they be able to make, or what degree of influence will they have in a decision-making process. It is also important to determine what level of input is going to be asked of them.

This chapter will look at:

- the various empowerment models and what we mean by 'representativeness'
- direct and indirect consultation methods
- what needs to be in place for effective participation
- current thinking on consulting with service users
- an overview of the Supporting People programme.

EMPOWERMENT MODELS

From an empowerment model perspective, user control can be measured to see how much real power both parties have. Arnstein's Ladder (1969) (Figure 1.1 below) is a model developed from citizen involvement in planning in the USA, which represents degrees of citizen participation and power as rungs up a ladder. Here, conflicts between both parties can lead to disempowerment and tokenism. Arnstein defines levels of non-participation as manipulation, therapy and informing; degrees of tokenism as informing, consultation and placation; and degrees of citizen power as partnership, delegated power and citizen control. This is a useful model for establishing how genuine your organisation is in the way it empowers service users: you can identify where on the ladder you see the staff and service users. It is adapted here to reflect service user involvement.

8   service user control

7   delegated power

6   partnership

5   placation

4   consultation

3   informing

2   therapy

1   manipulation

Figure 1.1 Arnstein's Ladder, adapted from citizen to service user, where from the top to the bottom of the ladder power shifts from the service user through tokenism to non-participation in relation to the professional

Historically, service users have often been asked for their views and an instant response has been required. What most of us usually need is time to deliberate and weigh up our thoughts and feelings in relation to a particular issue.

When considering strategic planning, service users may have no experience or understanding of the 'bigger picture' unless service providers take time to explain the information clearly. It is important that service users have time to understand the issues, and hear others' views, in order to make sense of complex information, weigh up a decision, and present a considered opinion. When discussing your strategy you need to recognise the value of a shared working practice preference of taking time to talk to service users to build empathy, communicate clearly and check their understanding of what you are asking. This is because it is quite a complex task to even ask the question: 'How would you like us to consult you in order to get your views on our services?'!

Representativeness and accountability

It would be helpful for you to discuss what would constitute service user representation for the purposes of your strategy and as part of any future models that could be developed. Representativeness can mean either statistical or democratic representativeness.

Statistical representativeness is where you are looking at the proportion or sample size of people whom you would need to ask for their views, in order to be confident that their views could be generalised to the whole population of service users in your agency.

Democratic representativeness refers to the ability of individuals (for example, on committees and in discussion groups) to reflect the views of a wider group. This could happen within your agency, or inter-agency, as a partnership with other providers or with commissioners. This has been a key topic in the Hampshire Model discussed later in the book, where a group of service users offer their views in a meeting format, and in between meetings seek the views of other service users. These views are then collated and fed to the County Core Group, the highest decision-making body for Supporting People in Hampshire.

Representative of...or being typical

Even if your target group(s) of service users is very small, compared to those of other services or the majority of users of Supporting People housing-related support services, the value of information from these groups is still of great importance. Approximately 80 per cent of the current funding goes to services for older people and those with learning disabilities, and the other 20 per cent is given for all those other services providing for the hard-to-reach groups.

Research has found that there is a high level of consistency in the views and values of service users, so that findings from smaller groups and from studies undertaken elsewhere can safely be used to guide action.

You also need to think about the fact that within each of your service user groups there were sub-groups and differing individuals making up the community – subsets, in terms of the Supporting People population, and again a subset of the general public. Consequently, it is likely that such diverse groups will find it hard to agree on appropriate individual(s) to represent them. In the authors' experience, consultation methods often favoured the articulate, active and confident. You then have two issues:

1. Which methods favour the less confident and articulate, and how can we use them?

2. If only confident and articulate service users get involved in consultation methods, how can we ensure that they represent the views of other service users?

Historically, it has been important to support the means by which the representatives can engage in a dialogue with their wider group (through meetings, a newsletter or a website, for example).

Clearly, however, it is much harder to obtain engagement with individuals who do not easily fit into an organised group or who choose not to conform to a group at all. Difficulties have been found in trying to consult with individuals receiving floating support, for example, where they do not necessarily meet with each other or fit any organised collective body. Consequently, the authors have found that, rather than trying to make them fit, it is better to use methods that respect the individual. Views can be sought on a one-to-one basis in person or by telephone, for example, and the results pooled.

Having said that, however, a one-off letter 'out of the blue' tends to end up in the bin, so service users need to be involved over a period of time in order to:

*   develop an understanding of the structures and processes they are engaged in
*   contribute to evolving plans
*   see the achievements and outcomes of their involvement.

Users who have acquired skills, confidence and knowledge through their participation are no longer considered 'typical' of the 'ordinary' user, but to have become 'professionalised'. 'Professional' is a positive attribute when applied to paid workers, but is used to invalidate the contribution of service users. For example, social workers heading up a care leavers' project were concerned that young peoples' representatives had become so well trained and professional that they had almost become 'mini staff'. Social workers were concerned that these representatives risked losing touch with those young people they were supposed to be representing. Alternatively, perhaps they developed a higher level of skill than they previously had to represent their former peers…

CONSULTATION METHODS

There are various guides to consultation methodologies for service users such as the Department of Transport and Regions (DTR) *Developing Good Practice in Tenant Participation – Housing* (Cole, Hickman, Millward and Reid 1999), the Housing Corporation's *Just Do It!* (Keeble 2000), a directory of examples of service users' involvement in supported housing, and their *Directory of Tenant and Resident Involvement Information* (2001) in CD format.

Ideas for good practice in generic service user involvement are well documented in *User Involvement – Principles and Practice for Involving Users in the Design and Delivery of Public Services* (Hope and Hargreaves 1997). These ideas are positive and suggest an ethos of commitment by professionals in developing an empowering organisation that supports and enables involvement of service users at all levels.

The following methods have generally been accepted as useful and helpful to service users.

Direct methods

- recruiting their support workers
- setting up a user involvement interest group
- developing a network of users
- constructing a register of users
- involving users in writing support plans
- training users to represent their own interests
- involving users in training staff.

Indirect methods

- improving publicity and information about services
- providing telephone helplines
- supporting development of resource centres for users
- aiding users to form groups.

WHAT NEEDS TO BE IN PLACE FOR EFFECTIVE PARTICIPATION?

Clearly we need to support, respect and empower service users so that they can take part in consultation or become involved to a greater degree in a service. In addition, the structure, culture and responsibilities of the organisation must be considered so that there is:

- senior management involvement, with identified senior managers having clear responsibility for working at strategic level to ensure that participation is integrated effectively into commissioning

- access to staff with sufficient skills and confidence to undertake involvement activities and develop credibility with outside organisations
- a positive organisational culture
- effective mechanisms for making good use of the team's knowledge, and ensuring that messages from service users and the public are fed into the organisation
- a system of enabling service users to understand the expectations on each 'side'.

An example of encouraging participation

Swindon People First (SPF) is a user-run self-advocacy group run by and for adults with learning difficulties (www.swindonpeoplefirst.org.uk).

SPF have drawn up an agreement for any organisations that would like them to take part in committee meetings.

Box 1.1 Swindon People First Contract

If you want People First to be on your committee you must agree these things to make it OK for us:

- We should have a voice to say what we want.
- You need to listen to us and give us time to talk.
- We will not come to your committee just so it looks good.
- You need to let us know why you want us on the committee.
- You need to tell us what we will get out of being on your committee.
- You have got to make minutes and agendas on tape if we want them.
- The committee should pay for a supporter.
- Everyone on the committee needs to be trained to know how to involve us.
- The committee has to use words we understand.
- We must be able to stop meetings if we need you to say something again or explain it.
- Everyone should have their expenses paid.
- If the rest of the committee get paid then we should too.

What resources will you need?

A Health Advisory Service review based on reports, site visits, surveys and current literature suggests that adequate resources (time, money, support, and staff time) are one of the factors most likely to promote successful user involvement. The review recommends the following.

- Employ salaried user involvement workers whose role is to collect, collate and interpret information on opinions, wishes and needs.

- Development workers can also stimulate or coordinate actions by groups of users or carers.

- Create user and carer initiative grants, so that essential costs can be covered, e.g. carers may not be able to attend meetings if they have to leave the person they are caring for alone.

- Train users and generally give them the time they need to develop knowledge and skills.

- Secure the mainstream funding you need from health and local authorities incorporated within strategic plans. You will need funding to cover: facilities (bases, office space, administrative and secretarial support); transport, personal expenses, setting-up network registers and helplines; and the costs to carers of people to substitute for them.

- Ensure that funding is predictable and ongoing.

(Firth and Kerfoot 1997)

What are the training needs of service users?

Ross (1995) interviewed more than 200 service users in 19 daycare centres across three local authority areas, and gathered the views of 150 users and carers through independent user forums.

Service users felt that training was fundamental to their ability to participate meaningfully and actively in service planning and delivery. Their training requirements included:

- assertiveness
- confidence building
- group work and committee skills.

The research found that involvement depended on staff commitment to users taking part, and their willingness to accompany and support users (Ross 1995).

The focus of the majority of the literature reviewed tends to be on tenants and/or relatively stable recipients of supported housing services, rather than the hard-to-reach groups defined in this project.

The former Office of the Deputy Prime Minister (ODPM) defined four levels at which service users can and should be making contributions:

1. Dialogue/information – this includes how service users are presented with information about the service and in the service, and includes literature that goes out from the service.

2. Day-to-day – simple and low-level decision-making on things that affect service users on a daily basis, such as food, décor and rules.

3. Planning and policy – this includes involvement in policy development, staff recruitment and medium-term planning.

4. Service management – this includes some involvement in how the service is run and managed and may include how users are involved at board level in decision-making, e.g. about future service developments.

Supporting People: A Guide to User Involvement for Organisations Providing Housing Related Services (Office of the Deputy Prime Minster (ODPM) 2003) examines methods for most client groups at the four levels, but does not provide focus for the hard-to-reach groups, or for consulting at the strategic level.

CONSULTING WITH 'HARD-TO-REACH' SERVICE USERS

Housing-related support services are available to vulnerable individuals in need of help to develop or sustain independent living.

Clearly there are large numbers of people who fall into the definition of 'those in need or receipt of statutory services', such as older people, those with enduring mental illness, learning disability, or physical disability. These people may be easier to reach via statutory services but may be harder to engage with or communicate with. One example of this is in learning disability services, or where symbols, pictures, diagrams or flow-charts are used for daily communication. These tools may also be appropriate for people who have literacy problems, or are dyslexic, or the tools may just make the point better than written language.

We hope that the methods and suggestions in this book can be used and adapted to suit the needs of any individuals you work with, in order to get them as meaningfully involved as possible in consultation processes.

What do we mean by 'vulnerable'?

'Vulnerability' is a term open to interpretation and users of housing-related support services may define themselves as 'vulnerable', or in need, to a greater or lesser extent.

A vulnerable adult is defined as someone who:

> is in need of community care services by reason of mental or other disability, age, or illness; and who is or may be unable to take care of him or herself, or unable to protect him or herself against significant harm or exploitation. (Department of Health 1999)

Historically, people have fallen through the net and have certainly not received the statutory care services they needed, and often the voluntary sector has provided this essential support. Ideally, of course, the voluntary and statutory sectors should work in partnership to ensure that the person in question receives the services they both need and want. We should take the same approach when engaging service users in strategies for consultation and involvement, and the book will demonstrate good examples of how this can happen.

You may be working with one, some, or all of the groups listed here:

- homeless people
- women escaping domestic violence
- people with drug/substance or alcohol addictions
- offenders, ex-offenders or those at risk of offending
- young people
- people from black and minority ethnic (BME) groups.

'Hard to reach' is defined as not having contact with statutory services, and also having no fixed address. Service users may be hard to reach because:

- they are not seen as fulfilling statutory requirements
- they have excluded themselves
- their primary contact has been with voluntary sector agencies.

In other words, our hard-to-reach service users fulfil at least one of these criteria:

1. transitory
2. not directly in criteria for local authority care
3. excluded by services, or have excluded themselves e.g. runaways.

These individuals or (more often) labelled groups such as 'addicts' are also usually regarded as unpopular by UK media standards, and hard to work with by social care and health standards, as they often have chaotic lives and are not necessarily compliant or predictable. They may also consider themselves to be socially excluded or have 'an inability to participate effectively in economic, social and political and cultural life, alienation and distance from mainstream society' (a Supporting People definition).

You may also find that you have service users who are generally seen as 'hard to reach' because they are:

- a potential user of a housing-related support service
- someone currently using this service
- someone who has recently 'moved on' to independence.

Current thinking on consultation with this group

To date, limited research has been undertaken on consulting with hard-to-reach service users, and in particular there is a 'near absolute absence of studies of service user involvement in a homelessness context specifically' (Velasco 2001).

Relevant research projects have been undertaken in specific areas.

- The Joseph Rowntree Foundation, renowned for their work into social exclusion, have produced papers addressing issues such as increasing user involvement and control in the voluntary sector (Bewley and Glendinning 1994, Ward 1997). Some of these describe key issues such as personal contact positively affecting consultation exercises for marginalised groups, and the difficulties in involving users at higher levels of strategic planning.

- The Community Care legislation specified a requirement for health, social services, the independent sector providers and service users to develop services appropriate to need by working together. Guidance in working towards developing user-led services is documented in Begum and Gillespie-Sells (1994).

- The National User Involvement Project was established in order to widen the range of service users involved in commissioning decisions and included those from BME groups and older people, as well as those with mental health problems and learning difficulties.

In January 1999 the Evaluation of the National User Involvement Project was published. This showed that there was a gap in 'understanding of the key access needs (Lindow 1999), for these groups to be able to become involved in terms of information formats and cultural practices. It was also found that users of services were still more involved in general planning than decision-making, and that service users needed a range of support and training in order to participate as fully as possible. This subsequent research shows that this is still an issue for commissioners of Supporting People.

As stated above, surveys where marginalised groups are the primary focus (especially homeless people) are scarce. The charity Groundswell UK appears to be the only well-known vehicle that consistently campaigns to raise awareness of issues for homeless people, as seen by homeless people. Groundswell has also produced the *Toolkit for Change* (1997).

You might like to start by holding workshops with service users where you can raise relevant topics and discuss definitions, for example:

- what 'user-led' really means
- management practices and approaches
- representation
- power
- valuing users and communication.

This can then eventually contribute to the formation of guidance and good practice principles for your agency.

It would be very useful for you to link with your service's commissioners (in partnership rather than fear!) to ensure that all parties understand the key access needs for your users to be able to become involved in terms of information formats and cultural practices.

The Evaluation of the National User Involvement Project (January 1999) also found that service users are still more involved in general planning than decision-making, and that they need a range of support and training in order to participate as fully as possible.

WHAT ARE THE ENABLERS AND BARRIERS TO CONSULTATION?

An action research study that distinguished between the concepts of 'user-centred user involvement' and 'management-centred user involvement' in voluntary organisations found that there were key enablers of change and key barriers to progress.

Enablers included consistent commitment by supportive and facilitative leaders who opened up structures for service users and encouraged relationship development.

Barriers included slow progress, varying commitment levels and varying availability of resources.

(Robson, Begum and Lock 2003).

We will look at enablers and barriers to consultation in more detail in Chapter 3.

THE SUPPORTING PEOPLE PROGRAMME

As the former ODPM grant was made available to look at consultation for Supporting People, it is useful to outline this programme here, for those unfamiliar with it.

Supporting People is designed to enable vulnerable people to achieve and maintain independence through the use of housing-related support services. In order to ensure that services are flexible to meet the needs of the individual, service users need to be at the centre of the support planning process. As part of a process of becoming an independent individual, able to contribute and function within a community, it is important for clients to feel that they have a voice and a valid contribution to make. Bringing together a group of people to achieve their goals can also be a cohesive and powerful force in itself.

Consultation in Supporting People

The Supporting People Quality Assurance Framework (QAF) reflects the merging demands of the Housing Corporation, Audit Commission, Best Value, and other bodies that all require demonstrable influence of service users in housing-related support services.

But, if quality is more than just compliance with externally set performance indicators, a more inside-out approach is needed by an organisation. Due to the pressures of time, money, skills and other considerations, organisational leadership is essential to devise a meaningful strategy of service user consultation. This consultation must be able to demonstrate not only compliance with these external standards, but also commitment to continuous improvement and real quality of service for clients.

Although this is not a book about leadership *per se*, without this coming from somewhere agencies will founder or fail. Quality management has to be led from the top with solid belief, not lip service. In turn, staff have to recognise where changes need to be made in working practice and procedure. There is more about this in Chapter 3.

Levels of service user consultation in Supporting People

As previously mentioned, the former ODPM defined four levels at which service users can and should be making contributions, and produced a *Guide to User Involvement for Organisations Providing Housing Related Support Services* providing clear guidance and examples of good practice for all levels (ODPM 2003a). The four levels are defined as:

1. Dialogue/information – this includes how service users are presented with information about the service and in the service and includes literature that goes out from the service.

2. Day-to-day – simple and low-level decision-making on things that affect service users on a daily basis, such as food, décor and rules.

3. Planning and policy – this includes involvement in policy development, staff recruitment and medium-term planning.

4. Service management – this includes some involvement in how the service is run and managed and may include how users are involved at board-level decision-making e.g. about future service developments.

Service user involvement is integral to the QAF, and higher grades are awarded to projects that can provide evidence of a greater degree of service user involvement.

Strategic planning for Supporting People

Barnes and his research team (Barnes and Wistow 1995, cited in Barnes and Wistow 1997) identified areas within which 'user control' can be exercised. These areas included the former ODPM's four levels, plus the fifth of strategic planning for Supporting People. Here Barnes includes elements of day-to-day service and management contact and planning, as well as:

- committee management and policy development
- local-authority-wide and inter-agency management and policy development
- national policy development.

You should aim to engage your service users in these first four levels initially, and we are sure that you are already some way there, as you have picked up this book! You can also enable your service users to participate at the fifth level. At this level, they should be able to contribute their views to the highest level of planning Supporting People services, through engagement with commissioners and having their views taken into account in the planning and prioritising of Supporting People services. There may not be a mechanism for this to happen yet in your area, but you could suggest it!

Currently, under Supporting People, the county inclusive forum would be the place for high-level strategic planning, although these decisions are subject to alteration at the local level, by district inclusive forums.

One commissioner interviewed as part of this project suggested that, in fact, 'the real decisions are taken by the Strategic Housing Officers Group', which includes people from the Government Office for the South East (GOSE) and the Housing Corporation, a local government officers' group, and not formally part of the Supporting People structure at all.

District inclusive forums make the local strategic plans, but clients may only have limited access to these. In most areas, clients are only involved in some of the set of working groups that most areas operate, which tend to deal with learning disabilities, physical disabilities, mental health and domestic violence.

On the Isle of Wight, such groups include young people who feed into the inclusive forum, strategic core group and then the council, as well as other linked strategies.

Commonly primary care trusts (PCT) and health authorities have their own systems of consultation, and local authorities may have other consultation frameworks with greater or lesser coordination, overlap and information exchange.

We need to make a distinction, however, between clients contributing their views as part of the regular activity of receiving a service, and their special attendance or involvement in consultation exercises for strategic planning. For the latter, you need to address the issue of pay and reward for participation, and various suggestions appear throughout this book.

Recent strategic-level consultation reviewed

Watson et al. (2003, p.34) reviewed the impact of Supporting People on the planning for housing and support for marginalised groups. Here the defined groups were:

- people with complex needs
- people who were high risk or presented a risk to themselves or others (through offending behaviour, drugs and alcohol, and mental health problems)

- people who were at risk from others (for instance, women escaping domestic violence)
- people who are hard to reach or hard to find.

'Hard-to-reach' people in this case were defined as those resistant to services or those who had been excluded from services (e.g. long-term homeless people). 'Hard-to-find' people included those in BME groups with little or no connection with formal care services, or hidden homeless, such as young people 'sofa surfing' (permanently living in different temporary accommodation with friends or family).

The study found that, despite the policy commitment by Supporting People to the housing and support of marginalised groups, at a local level there had been the more immediate pressures of the transitional period to contend with. Although keen to pursue improvements for the above marginalised groups the study raised evident concern about the level of availability of resources to do so in the short term.

Hackney Borough Council (Hackney Supporting People Team 2003) has already written a draft strategy for user involvement to cover consulting with service users at a strategic level i.e. about best value, homelessness strategy and Supporting People. This strategy clarifies what is and is not consultation, and cites examples of consultation processes that can be used at the individual, scheme and strategy level, including the inclusive forum, Hackney Service User Group and an annual 'Speak Out' event. Hackney Borough Council's strategy highlights the importance of asking how people would like to be consulted, and proposing other methods that could be used, such as 'e'-conferencing, road shows and focus groups.

The Supporting People programme appears to be committed to going out to visit other meetings and events rather than expecting people to come to them, and there is a focus on the inclusion of BME groups, and cultural sensitivity. This is so far only apparent in the review process where service users are sent questionnaires and asked via providers whether or not they would like to be interviewed as part of a Supporting People service review. There is, however, little explicit mention of how to engage with hard-to-reach service users specifically.

SUMMARY

This chapter considered:

- the various empowerment models and what is meant by 'representativeness'
- direct and indirect consultation methods

- what needs to be in place for effective participation
- current thinking on consulting with service users
- an overview of the Supporting People programme.

Although the research undertaken in this area is plentiful for tenant participation, it is increasingly scarce for hard-to-reach service users, and almost totally absent in terms of service users' preferred methods of consultation for strategic decision-making.

It does not matter whether or not the Supporting People programme is funding your service, as you can transfer, adapt and apply all our findings for any organisation and client group where service user consultation can be improved.

We hope that this has started you off thinking about the different strands to service user consultation and involvement, and that you will find the following workbook helpful.

Workbook

Where are you now?

The following exercises and questions will help you work towards a comprehensive strategy for service user involvement, including policy, procedures and methods.

This first section enables you and your team or organisation to clarify who your users are and how you currently work. The questions may be answered individually or used as the basis of a team discussion at any level of an organisation.

Exercise

- Use Arnstein's Ladder as a discussion tool for a team meeting (see Figure 1.1, page 22).
- Where do you consider your organisation to be on Arnstein's Ladder?
- Do your staff agree with the placing?
- Would your service users agree?

Focus your mind:

- How are services structured and service users distributed in your organisation?

Now start thinking:

- Do you rely on the structure to dictate your methods of involvement, e.g. only having house meetings when they are convenient, or thinking you cannot consult with individuals receiving floating support as you cannot get them together?
- Do people actually need to come together to give their views?
- How could house meetings become more popular as a tool for consultation?

Evidencing your work:

- How do you currently measure the quality of the service you provide?
- How do you evidence service user involvement currently?

Consulting with service users:

- What methods have you used to consult with service users in the past?
- How successful have these been?
- Who are the hard-to-reach service users in your community/covered by your agency's services?

Exercise

Here is a planning tool devised for you to look at where your organisation is now in terms of consultation and the standard you eventually want to achieve (see Table 1.1). Use it to start thinking about how well service users are currently consulted for each of the four levels listed in the left-hand columns. Note what you already do well, what needs working on, and where there are gaps that need filling, so that you end up with a clearer picture about what needs to be done in the future.

Table 1.1 Needs analysis

Level	Good	Needs work	Gap
Information			
Day-to-day			
Development and policy			
Management			
Strategic planning (contributing to local Supporting People strategies or other statutory programmes)			

CHAPTER 2

The ROCC Research Project

INTRODUCTION

This chapter gives an overview of the ROCC project, including the purpose and goals of the project, the research parameters and the main findings, including successes and failures. The aim of this chapter is to lend validity to the rest of the book. The authors have put theory and practice into action to show how service users can be meaningfully engaged in consultation processes, however hard to reach those users may be.

BACKGROUND TO THE PROJECT

ROCC is a Hampshire-based charity providing advice, support, representation, consultancy and training for supported housing organisations. ROCC initially stood for Resettlement of Offenders Coordinating Committee, but as it gradually widened its field of reference it came to be known simply as ROCC.

The former Office of the Deputy Prime Minister (ODPM) funded a piece of action research in 2002–03 to look at consulting with hard-to-reach service users for strategic decision-making under the Supporting People programme (ODPM 2003). This was deemed an important piece of work, as the ODPM saw the service user as central to the housing-related support services that he or she receives, and believed that these services should be flexible and responsive to the individual's needs.

Service user involvement is a core value for the Supporting People programme, and a service's quality is scored on the extent to which service users' views are involved in all aspects of the service planning and delivery. This piece of work was ahead of its time, as many services were struggling with the notion of evidencing service user involvement at lower levels.

Purpose of the project

Initially the purpose of the project was to trial different consultation methods for strategic decision-making for Supporting People with hard-to-reach clients in Hampshire, Southampton, Portsmouth and the Isle of Wight. The purpose changed when the authors realised that merely asking people *how* they would like to be consulted took a significant amount of time, due to the complexity of the issues and barriers; so they concentrated on this, rather than on trialling their own ideas and methods.

Due to the time and resources available, the authors did not include refugees and asylum seekers as a target group *per se*, although some may have formed part of the other groups they spoke with. However, the findings and methods described in the book may be just as applicable to refugees and asylum seekers, although some other considerations may need to be taken into account, such as language and cultural differences.

During the process, the authors drew on individual experiences from these hard-to-reach groups and asked them for their preferred methods of consultation for strategic planning for the Supporting People programme. The authors then used this material to create good practice guidance for clients, service providers and commissioners.

FEEDBACK AND LEVELS OF INVOLVEMENT

Clients told the authors that they felt that the organisations that provided housing-related support services for them did usually consult with the clients about daily decisions and planning in the short term.

However, most organisations of which the service users who were consulted had experience rarely included service users in the higher-level organisational management or strategic planning decision-making processes. Those organisations that did consult with their users at these higher levels tended to do so very well, as attested by their clients.

Motivation

The authors discussed with the clients issues of motivation for and against taking part in consultation processes, and the clients developed a model that could be used to inform service providers and commissioners.

The clients' model proposed that both an interest in strategic planning and the ability to contribute to the process tended to develop when clients had moved out of a crisis period, and were more settled.

Having said this, clients felt that day-to-day consultation could inform longer-term planning, provided the organisation sought information in ways that clients were happy with, or by methods that provided a direct benefit to clients through the act of undertaking them. For example, service users learning how to put together a newsletter for their organisation develop new skills and confidence through undertaking the process. The content of such a newsletter is often designed to communicate and consult with service users about issues they may be interested in, and feed back results of such consultations.

Many of the people interviewed were cynical about the processes and value of consultation, and wanted organisations to demonstrate respect for them and their individual needs, if they were to participate in strategic planning exercises.

Both commissioners and service users shared the opinion that consultation should take place where service users felt at most ease, i.e. 'on their own turf'. Most people, whether they were users, providers or commissioners of services, were open to trying more creative ways of gaining information, such as better use of email, access to websites, or creative writing projects, and would prefer these methods rather than the sole use of formalised meetings.

Commissioners

It was important for commissioners of housing-related support services (i.e. those paying for the services) that they received what they could perceive as accurate and valid data about service users' views, and that this should be gained as independently as possible from service providers. The authors made a proposition to develop a model that would allow consistent standards to be maintained for client involvement. This proposal is included later in the book (Chapter 7).

Cost

As another thread to the research, the authors explored the cost of service user involvement and developed a planning guide, which is presented later in the book (Chapter 8).

Most people agreed that, benefits issues aside, clients should be offered payment or reward for participating in consultation relating to strategic planning, if this activity formed an addition to their usual daily lives. If this participation continued, again service users wanted to be paid or rewarded in some way. Clients also felt it would be useful for organisations to consult them about how they would like to be paid or rewarded, as individuals preferred different things. Two alternative examples of rewards identified by the authors were a letter of reference that could help in future employment, or the issue of vouchers for use in retail outlets so they could, for example, buy themselves books or CDs.

Organisations can carry out independent consultation under the Supporting People programme by using relevant existing structures, such as those networks currently provided by Connexions and Social Cohesion Units for young people and black and minority ethnic (BME) groups.

However, as a result of the research, the authors have proposed a new model that would be independent of any statutory agency. (The model is examined in more detail in Chapter 5.)

Two local authorities have already successfully adopted this model specifically for Supporting People, and the University of Portsmouth has also adapted it to engage users of social and care services in the new social work degree.

STARTING THE ROCC RESEARCH

In order to conduct the work, it was important to look at what was understood by the term 'consultation' and undertake some desktop research in this area. Here the nature of consultation with hard-to-reach service users is examined, in particular at the level of strategic planning for Supporting People in light of the literature.

It ought to be stressed here that this project was not a piece of research that had a hypothesis that the authors were trying to prove or disprove. The main concern was asking people what they thought, and then making sense of it.

Research results are generally only seen to be valid if they are taken from a large-enough sample for the proposition being examined. In this case the authors were constrained by time, money, and all the potential barriers (such as wary service users); so consultants spoke to as many people as possible, across as many services as possible, in the defined geographical area. The authors emphasise that they have taken the results from the findings of those they spoke to, and have tried not to make generalisations unless they can be substantiated.

Before the research started, it was important to establish the parameters and the methods that would be used to obtain the required information.

Research parameters

The parameters of the project were set partly by the funder (former ODPM) and partly by the ROCC director who had secured the grant, Beth Taylor, the project manager, the steering group and consultant group. It was obvious that it would not be possible to talk to everyone in all groups in all areas of

Hampshire. Accordingly, it was agreed that the authors would take at least a small sample of each of the chosen groups, ideally in each geographical area, and in a way that was likely to put the service users at ease.

This project was funded as a piece of action research with the intention that different consultation methods could be tried, tested and adapted in the light of feedback. The process was designed to be developmental and organic, and created a wealth of learning and development for all the participants – clients, service providers, consultant fieldworkers and commissioners.

The geographical area to be covered was Hampshire, designated as an 'excellent' local authority by the government, and included New Forest, Test Valley, Basingstoke, Hart, Rushmoor, Aldershot, East Hampshire, Winchester, Havant, Fareham, Gosport and Eastleigh. Also included were the unitary authorities of Southampton, Portsmouth and the Isle of Wight.

What is consultation?

The ROCC research project adopted the ethos that clients should be offered the opportunity to be as fully consulted as is meaningfully possible, in all aspects of the Supporting People services they receive. The idea was to use service users' views to assist in strategic planning in order to develop and improve the services.

For the purposes of the ROCC research, the authors decided to focus on the principle of consultation, and our challenge was to see how service users could be effectively consulted for strategic decision-making under Supporting People. Arguably, the more effective the consultation methods, the more involved service users might become in the process. Service users would also need to be 'involved' by giving their thoughts on how they would like to be consulted, with a view to setting up effective and creative mechanisms for the most excluded groups in our community.

So when looking at involvement it was important to be able to:

- give out information about the research project
- consult users about their preferred methods
- decide on workable models together
- act together to provide a framework for consultation at the strategic level.

Each organisation or commissioner may need to take a view on the degree of power that clients are genuinely allowed to have in order to effectively develop consultation methodologies for strategic planning. This can be facilitated by deciding *whether or not* they want clients to participate, be consulted with, or be empowered.

Providing information

Giving information was a good starting point to engaging service users in the ROCC research project on consultation strategies. Just giving information on its own may be appropriate when:

- there is a legal requirement to do so and there is no negotiation, e.g. on health and safety issues
- you want to get a message across but do not require feedback or comment
- you are initiating a process, and people need information to become involved at a later stage.

It was important, however, for the project team to ensure that all the involved parties were clear about what was needed for the project, and how people could get involved, as support from service providers in putting us in touch with service users was imperative.

Fieldwork

It was agreed that the majority of the fieldwork should take place in day-centre type settings for the following reasons.

- We should go out to clients, not expect them to come to us.
- The majority of hard-to-reach people had a presence here, e.g. multicultural centres, homelessness day centres, drugs and alcohol drop-in centres, and other locations.
- Individuals might be more forthcoming if they were not interviewed within a service where they held a tenancy (as far as this was possible).
- Drop-in type centres are not directly funded to provide housing-related support services, although they often fulfil essential needs.
- Refuges for women escaping violence generally try to maintain confidentiality of address as far as possible.

(See also the Swindon 'People First' contract on page 26.)

Due to the difficulties in getting, developing and maintaining contact, participation and trust with hard-to-reach service users, the authors eventually decided to ask clients about their previous experiences of consultation, and how they would like to be consulted for strategic decision-making for Supporting People, and to do this as informally as possible, so as to put people at ease. It was agreed that this approach would replace the goal of trialling methods of consultation because, after much discussion, it was felt that the latter was inappropriate as a first intervention. The authors wanted to ask service users what worked for them, as well as look for examples of different methods that service providers had used successfully, with a view to publicising them.

With this new approach in mind, the authors selected consultants with experience of working with particular groups, such as homeless people, those with alcohol and substance issues, people with a history of offending, and people with mental health problems. Individual consultants arranged to meet with service users on a one-to-one basis, in informal groups, and in pre-arranged focus groups, with the assistance of service providers.

One consultant reported that, when he visited some day centres, clients he had previously worked with recognised him. This was fortunate, because these clients then allowed him to interview them and encouraged others to talk to him who might well not have done so otherwise.

One female consultant had recently completed a piece of work consulting with single homeless women, including those who had experienced domestic violence. She was sensitive to the fears that these women have about being found by abusive partners, and was able to speak with individuals and small groups both in and out of refuge settings, as agreed by staff and the women who consented to be interviewed.

These consultants spent time chatting to service users, explaining terms and issues of confidentiality, and getting to know about them as far as was reasonably possible in the time available, in order to build rapport and some trust.

One consultant undertook more formalised one-to-one interviews with a sample of commissioners of Supporting People services. His brief was slightly different: to identify how commissioners valued consultation with service users, what impact this might have on decisions made, how commissioners might like to consult with service users, and in what forms they would be prepared to receive views from them, e.g. organised questionnaires, focus groups, or ongoing telephone lines, email, etc.

Additionally, discussions were to be held about the manner of consulting service users independent of their service providers.

The authors also took informal opportunities to seek views from young people, including conversations with them struck up at events attended by the project manager, such as the Hampshire Teenage Pregnancy Partnership, where young mothers and young people from the Youth Council were in attendance.

In the absence of a specialist in working with Roma and travellers, the project manager met with the Hampshire Gypsy and Traveller Liaison Officer (GLO) to discuss how best to consult with members of these groups. He helpfully suggested accompanying the project manager on site visits, as both acknowledged that the latter would not get a good response if he approached these groups unaccompanied.

This feeling was borne out by reality when the two of them arrived to conduct the work and it was apparent that members of these communities looked to the GLO to see whether or not they should take part in a meeting. The project manager was able to speak to some of the women on sites where they were available and willing and a service user from the good practice group (see below) spoke with the men.

Clearly Roma and travellers comprise smaller subgroups and ethnic origins and cannot be homogenised as one group, except perhaps in terms of their rights. At the time of writing this book, the right to remain and local authorities' lack of provision of temporary and permanent sites are topical in the news. (It is still the case that there is no imperative for local authorities to make temporary or permanent provision for travellers. Consequently local MPs are rarely if ever interested in taking up the cause.)

Views of service providers

An additional piece of work within the project was to seek views from service providers on the topic of service user consultation. As ROCC is a membership organisation, we decided to write to the members with a covering letter and questionnaire. The letter explained the purpose of the research and asked members to take a couple of minutes to complete the questionnaire and return it in confidence. Some members returned their questionnaire confidentially and others were happy to indicate which agency they were from. Questions covered the service user groups' service, consultation methods used, perceived barriers to consultation from staff and service users, and anything that worked particularly well.

Input groups

Three groups provided input to the project: the good practice group, the steering group and the consultants' group.

The good practice group

This was set up as a challenge group for the project and was a pilot joint working group. Membership was drawn from clients, commissioners and a service provider, and an independent and experienced consultant acted as facilitator. In terms of its development and achievements, this was the most interesting group, as there was a lot of individual sharing of experiences, and commissioners stated that they found the experience immensely rewarding because they were encouraged by the service users to 'be themselves', which in turn improved group trust.

The group was able to undertake tasks on behalf of the project, such as reviewing a draft vulnerability protocol for a local council, and drafting letters to tenants explaining rent changes under Supporting People. Some individuals also took the opportunity to visit drug agencies to seek views and advertise the project, and members also helped devise the questionnaire format for interviewing commissioners, and assisted with some of the fieldwork, e.g. interviewing Roma and travellers with the project manager.

The steering group

The steering group consisted of representation from Supporting People, service providers and users and the then chair of the ROCC Board, Simon Mantle. The role of this group was to ensure that the project met deadlines and to enable progress as problems arose, which could then be discussed. In consultation with clients, the group drew up a list of values as a commitment for all individuals involved in the project, but particularly for professionals to be mindful of their perceived power, and also of the importance and value of input from service users.

The consultants' group

All the consultants working on the project were invited to meet at the early stages of the project development to communicate their views on approaches and methods, then later to share information about fieldwork progress.

Communications

Inter-group communication was the project manager's responsibility and he attended the steering group and consultants' group and liaised with the facilitator of the good practice group.

The ROCC membership was a good starting point for advertising and gaining commitment to the project, as it included organisations that provide housing-related support services for vulnerable people, including our hard-to-reach groups across the designated region.

The organisations were also used as access points to hard-to-reach service users, as staff members from these organisations could pass on information to service users, both verbally and in poster form.

The project manager wrote an informal 'Dear Diary' column, which was posted monthly on the ROCC website (www.rocc.org.uk). Hard copies (print-outs) of the column were also sent out in the ROCC monthly mailings. To make it more interesting visually, graphics were added by members of a homeless service-user-led IT project that operates IT training for homeless people in Portsmouth. In this way the authors communicated the progress of the project and requested responses or interest on an ongoing basis.

When the fieldwork and desktop research was completed, the project manager drafted a final report, with editorial support from the current chief executive of ROCC, Nichola Goom. Finally, the project manager presented the report to the former ODPM.

SUCCESSES AND FAILURES OF THE PROJECT

What follows is a summary of what worked well and what didn't. This summary is for the benefit of anyone thinking of doing a similar piece of work, whether you are planning to conduct some research, or a project such as planning your service user involvement strategy! The authors have illustrated their collective learning throughout the book and included other findings where appropriate.

Successes?

The project was completed on time and within budget. The director had planned an appropriate budget and timescale, and the authors only received money on completion of various outputs. This was an incentive to get the job done!

The authors kept the sponsor at the former ODPM informed of their progress and discussed their proposed amendments with him, to gain his understanding and consequent support and approval to change the brief.

Consultants had clear contracts and timescales. This meant that they could combine their responsibilities on the project with their other work commitments at times that suited them, as they were all self-employed and flexible.

Communication was on the whole good within the various teams and with the ROCC membership, thanks to clear outlines of responsibility and an ethos of consultation within the project.

The authors consulted with over 160 hard-to-reach service users, and used their opinions and one of the authors' learning to develop a two-tier model of consultation to engage both the transient and the more settled in a meaningful way for providing data to Supporting People.

Failures?

Essentially the original project brief was not completed!

The authors changed the brief from trialling methods of consultation to see what worked, to consulting people about their preferred methods of consultation. This followed lengthy discussions of the issues, especially barriers to consultation, as the authors felt there was a risk of treating vulnerable people as experimental guinea pigs.

The authors were aware from the scant research up until that time, and from their own experiences of the work, that hard-to-reach people had higher priorities than being consulted for strategic planning. Therefore the authors felt that it was better to gather information about their previous experiences of consultation, and what they would have preferred, or would like to take part in, in the future. The authors believed that this was a successful decision, in that they made a good choice, negotiated the change and followed it through.

SUMMARY: MAIN FINDINGS

The findings are explored in more detail in the rest of the book, but here is a summary.

Barriers and enablers

The main findings were that a variety of factors presented barriers to service users and staff, and that the presence of other factors enabled better inclusion (see Chapter 3). Consequently any work to develop service user participation and consultation needs to include the development of staff as well as service users.

Creative methods

More creative methods than those traditionally used could be applied for mutual benefit to professionals and users. As service users go through different degrees of stability and instability in their lives, they considered some methods more attractive than others, and some useful activities could provide space for consultation on an informal basis.

The outcome: an effective two-tier model

From these findings, the authors developed a two-tier model of consultation. Hampshire and Portsmouth Supporting People teams have used this model effectively, and carers and users of social services involved with the social work degree at the University of Portsmouth have also adapted the model for their use.

This is the model.

- Service users (or recent service users) operate within a more formal setting, such as regular meetings, to discuss the main issues.

- The service users are then trained and supported to use less formal methods to consult with other service users who may be less able or willing to attend the formal groups.

This model provides a wider use of informal networks from which we can draw the views of service users, and it gives individuals the opportunity to be involved at their preferred level.

Over time the authors hope that enabling service users to consult with other service users will provide inspiration for those with less confidence, encouraging and empowering them to be involved in the process from consultation to inclusion, in or out of the formal structure.

CHAPTER 3

Barriers and Enablers to Effective Service User Consultation

INTRODUCTION

In this chapter we will look at:

- service users' motivation for participating in consultation
- barriers to consultation faced by service providers and service users and the reasons behind these barriers
- various case studies on motivating service users and developing policies.

HOW MOTIVATED ARE SERVICE USERS AND PROVIDERS?

There are overall similarities in motivation for service users and professional staff, in terms of their respective motivation and fears around the issue of service user consultation and its processes and outcomes.

Service users

Service users can be motivated by wanting to 'put something back', or directly benefit their personal development. Service providers expressed a motivation to empower service users in order that they could become more independent and as fully functioning community members as possible.

(A 'community' may be immediate and small scale, such as people living in a shared house, or refer to individuals living in the wider community as citizens.) In turn, service users can develop the confidence and skills to become better engaged in voluntary or paid work, training and development, as their curriculum vitae (CV) and job prospects expand.

Service users do, however, have reservations about taking part in consultation processes, sometimes expressly attributing these to previous negative experiences. The service users we met were wary of 'looking stupid' and not understanding jargon, and had sometimes felt that 'lip service' was paid to their views, or that they were not given feedback on topics they had given their views about.

The following case study is of particular interest because of its coded star system that enables tenants to assess the level of commitment required for certain consultation activities. This seems to be a useful method that could be adopted and/or adapted for use in other housing-related support services.[1]

Case study 3.1 Atlantic Housing Ltd: star code system for commitment

The Atlantic Housing Ltd employs a coded star system to help inform tenants about the level of commitment required for involvement with its tenants' group programmes. People live busy lives and many are completely in the dark when it comes to assessing the involvement needed in such schemes.

The star system is easy to absorb and uses a blue star grading system for the different levels of tenant participation. For instance, if you chose options such as absorbing the regular tenants' newspaper, suggestion box input, reading association publications, websites, local news sheets, letters and leaflets, etc., you would earn a single blue star – in other words a low level of commitment is required from the tenant.

As we move on to more demanding input levels the number of blue stars rises. For instance, joining the editorial panel of the tenants' newspaper requires an occasional meeting and input into any one of a number of creative aspects, including graphics, layout, feature selection, and contributing articles personally, so for this involvement you would earn two stars on the commitment scale.

Onwards and upwards. Three-star requirements place you as an active member of a residents' or tenants' group, attending several different types of meetings regularly and becoming quite seriously involved in the decision-making process that affects your community. Leisure and social activities may well also ensue and a reasonable level of commitment will be required in order to ensure that somebody makes a worthwhile contribution. If no tenants' group exists in a certain area, individuals can still join the three-star brigade by speaking for themselves and others in their areas at tenants' forums.

1   The processes relating to resident involvement at Atlantic Housing Limited have changed significantly since the time of writing, and are no longer current practice. For any updates or enquiries, please contact First Wessex Housing Group at www.firstwessexhg.co.uk.

The First Wessex Housing Group (FWHG)'s umbrella of forums includes established debate platforms within both geographical and specific needs arenas. Area forums exist alongside sheltered housing forums and FWHG is looking actively to develop further consultation forums in the near future. A 'young people's forum' is under current proposal alongside other supported housing projects.

Involvement within the three-star grading advises a medium level of commitment. From three to four blue stars and, suddenly, we enter what is classed as the 'high' level of commitment. At this level, tenants are offered the chance to work in a number of key areas, including BIG (the Business Improvement Group), who consult closely with FWHG Management in terms of spearheading improved business services and monitoring standards. Tenants will need to be able to commit to both daytime and night time meetings, whilst retaining a choice of which BIG projects they wish to become associated with.

In addition to BIG, four-star tenants can also become members of management and tenants' consultative groups, scrutinising policies and final documents before they are sent to the board for application. This again is a time-consuming commitment with regular varied meetings taking place night and day. Yet another area of input revolves around joining the tenants' inspection group. This group gives tenants the chance to work with staff in assessing quality of services, with feedback of the findings through the BIG channel. Once more there is an emphasis on daytime availability.

An examination of the FWHG standards for residents' groups shows a type of constitution that would probably protect against the type of atmosphere outlined at the opening of this section. This includes rigidly enforced equal opportunities policies, emphasis on open membership to all tenants and residents, and, very important, an annual review designed to ensure the group maintains these standards.

It is interesting to note, however, that, as the blue stars increase and the commitment levels demanded from tenants rise, the number of daytime meetings increases and the guidelines emphasise the availability of a tenant to attend these.

This does seem to underline the points made in the opening paragraphs. Whilst FWHG is appearing to make sincere efforts to apply an all-inclusive policy, there may still be fundamental problems with its system. These problems clash with the salient principles of the inclusive culture and are shared by countless organisations.

Outside specialist forums such as those for the elderly and young people in sheltered care, the rising emphasis on important daytime meetings means that a large, defined part of the community will be excluded. As a consequence, ironically, the more important the nature of business and involvement, the more likely it is that those in full-time employment are going to be excluded from the process, because their own work commitments are going to govern their lack of willingness and ability to apply for positions.

This aspect can have a dual effect – one being that many talented tenants with the relevant business acumen and skills may not get involved. As such, the community and the association providing the service are not being served to the best potential the process could achieve. Second, if there is a collective perception that a tenants' group and the host service provider are not inclusive of a large layer of the community, this could significantly damage their public image.

With its emphasis on annual review of all the relevant aspects, we are sure that FWHG will be able to identify and find solutions to what are common problems and no reflection of their individual system.

In fact, the FWHG system does appear to be well structured, earnest and comprehensive in both its design and application. Other housing groups could certainly learn from the depth and commitment FWHG brings to the inclusive culture and the high quality of its presentation literature. The star system in particular provides tenants with an easy-to-absorb guide to a field of work that can prove both interesting and rewarding in terms of genuine community-orientated service and achievement.

Service providers

Providers of housing-related support services have expressed worries about losing power or being 'taken over' by service users, if they were to engage in consultation processes. Clearly we need to reduce and tackle these fears in order to help remove other barriers and enable fuller participation in consultation processes.

BARRIERS TO CONSULTATION AT A STRATEGIC LEVEL

There are barriers to consultation at a strategic level as perceived by providers and clients; some may be shared and others more specific to the individual's role. This section explores in more detail some of the barriers faced by professionals and clients, and then addresses factors that can be used to better enable involvement in consultation processes.

Service providers – perceived barriers to effective service user consultation

At the outset of your strategy development, you can always send out anonymous questionnaires to staff and service users to ask the question: 'What barriers get in the way of having a service user consultation strategy?'

Comments from staff in our survey included:

- 'No one person (member of staff) has a specific remit.'
- 'Users get stuck in trivia and cannot see the whole picture.'
- 'Have tried various formats but cannot sustain (clients') interest.'
- 'The women have pressing needs now and no energy left for management issues.'
- 'Would need a crèche.'
- 'The meetings are barriers in themselves as they use jargon and are held at inaccessible times and venues.'
- 'Changing client group.'
- 'Hearing those who are not as vocal.'

If this is typical of the agencies in our geographical area then there are clear needs in terms of investment in time for staff and support for clients wanting to take part. There is also a clear admission that some professionals do not feel confident to embark on a strategy for service user consultation at a strategic level.

Although we know that some of these respondents were involving clients in consultation at lower levels, or trying to set up user panels, one member stated that they felt their organisation undertook very little consultation at any level, but recognised that it was an area that needed to be addressed. Some providers who responded said they did not know how to consult with service users, or qualified this by saying that they did not know how to do so 'effectively'.

It would seem from our experience and the literature that barriers faced by staff are practical issues in terms of time and money and resources, and affected by perceptions of service user motivation.

Robson, Locke and Dawson (1997) surveyed 42 voluntary sector organisations and found that over half the senior managers felt the biggest barrier to service user participation was the users' preferred interest in the quality of the service they received rather than 'management issues'. Other reported perceived barriers were: service users' state of mental health, lack of understanding of committee procedures, travelling problems, and lack of motivation.

Attitude

When examining these professional attitudes, it is worth considering which of these are real, and which imagined barriers, conscious decisions or subconscious attitudes born out of the fear of challenge or change.

If professionals have been of a mind to 'do to' rather than 'work with' clients, their very role, value and purpose are being confronted. It may take decidedly longer to assist clients to do something for themselves than doing it for them, whether that is making a phone call or a strategic decision. The value, however, is in the increase to clients' personal independence and development within the immediate or wider community.

It has been researched and borne out anecdotally by our research project that it is the staff working in housing-related support services that can put up barriers to inclusive work with clients. Sometimes staff do not feel sufficiently motivated themselves to promote the idea of empowering service users to meet their fullest potential. These barriers may include:

- fear of being taken over or losing control
- not being 'needed' in the same way
- lack of resources – time/money/knowledge
- perceived previous lack of interest from service users.

It has also been reported that certain staff may fear change, or feel sufficiently threatened to be unwilling to accept change readily. An example of this has been seen where a registered home for people with mental health problems was de-registered and the ethos of 'doing for' changed to 'supporting to do'. Staff faced the feeling that maybe they were being criticised for 'doing it wrong' for years, and fears that the service users could not cope without them, or feeling that they might have felt more comfortable in an environment where cooking for service users gave both parties a sense of wellbeing, whereas teaching another to cook could be slow and frustrating.

The attitude that does not recognise a client's capacity to develop and grow can only limit that growth and development, and engender a prejudiced view of what vulnerable people can and cannot achieve. If this is the case in the daily workplace, then it is bound to restrict the expectations of exactly what clients can be consulted about. We need to acknowledge and then challenge this resistance, so that we can develop genuinely useful structures that allow and respect a client's right to participate and be consulted.

Although policymakers have increasingly pushed for greater participation by clients and it is a requirement of Supporting People, it is better to have full and genuine support rather than lip service if the concept is to be meaningfully embedded in the planning and delivery of housing-related support services.

We need to allow time for any change management programme to be successful, and changing the thinking of both staff and service users to encourage them along the lines of service user consultation and involvement is no exception.

It is essential to:

- have strong and positive leadership of the organisation
- listen to concerns
- offer support, training and development for all parties
- use supervision and team meetings
- ensure communication is effective at all levels of the organisation
- ensure that if a member of staff is to have the responsibility to take this work forward, they are also given the necessary authority and budget.

Staff structures and jargon

You may hold your own assumptions and experiences that you might need to question in terms of the use of professional jargon, inherent structures, habits and expectations. We believe that it is only by being open to suggestion and change that you are going to be able to hear what clients have to say, in environments where they feel comfortable.

The following case study offers a good example of the importance of staff commitment in engaging in the process of service user consultation.

Case study 3.2 Worthing Churches Homeless Projects (WCHP) and service user involvement

In 2003 the trustees approved a statement that WCHP would work toward involving people who use their services in the ongoing delivery and development of the services they provide.

WCHP provides a direct access hostel, Stepping-Stones Project, day centre and community link team. These services have developed over a ten-year span with the day centre the most recent development. They engage over 500 individuals every year.

Over the years, WCHP has made efforts to consult with people who use its services. This consultation has taken the form of questionnaires, individual consultations, discussion groups and regular meetings. More recently, WCHP has made provision within its innovative support plan outcome monitoring, to quantify service users' own assessment of the organisation's contribution to the service users' achievement of their support plan goals.

However, it was felt that WCHP should encourage more constructive input and deeper ownership. The Service User Involvement Working Group was created to bring staff and users together. The group also includes one of the trustees and external input from the local Council for Voluntary Services. The terms of reference were agreed and cover observation, monitoring, information, review and recommendation. These functions focus on developing existing approaches and identifying new initiatives to ensure that service user involvement is meaningful across all WCHP areas of activity.

In addition to this strategic focus, there is the ongoing contribution to day-to-day practice, such as discussion and recommendation on policies and procedures, etc. WCHP is shortly to run an 'away day' with service users to look at how they would like to be developed or trained to take an active role in consultation exercises. Part of the day will focus on how to contribute to discussions effectively, and how to chair meetings.

WCHP feels it has made a positive start and is encouraged that this ongoing commitment will continue to see positive results as a culture of involvement and ownership is actively promoted amongst all stakeholder groups – both internal and external.

Interview by Helen Brafield with Don Moat, Chair of the
Service User Involvement Working Group, December 2004

Worthing Churches Homeless Projects has been kind enough to share its Service User Involvement Policy:

Box 3.1 Worthing Churches Homeless Projects

Registered Charity No: 1027832

Service User Involvement Policy

WCHP actively seeks to involve its service users in the ongoing delivery and development of services.

Monthly service user meetings are held in each area of the projects, St. Clare's Day Centre, the direct access hostel and the Stepping Stones Project. These meetings are widely advertised to service users, who are encouraged to attend and to take ownership of these meetings.

These meetings provide the opportunity to share reflections, concerns and ideas on the part of service users, staff and trustees. These meetings are minuted by staff, with copies of minutes circulated to service users, staff and senior management.

At least once a year service users are consulted regarding the strategic development of WCHP and its services.

In addition to these meetings, suggestion boxes are situated in areas easily accessible by service users in each of the projects. Suggestions are read out at each of the project's monthly staff meetings. These suggestions are discussed and minuted as part of the meeting. Copies of these meetings go to senior management.

Links with groups such as Groundswell (a national organisation promoting and developing self-help initiatives in the UK with people who are homeless, excluded or living in poverty) are encouraged at service user level and also at management level to inform the development of WCHP's service user involvement. A WCHP trustee has specific responsibility to help oversee and develop service user involvement within WCHP. Service user involvement as an issue in itself is an ongoing consideration in the development of WCHP's strategy.

In addition to the above, WCHP encourages service users to be aware of WCHP's client grievance procedure. This procedure has been designed to offer service users the greatest amount of support possible. It is therefore essential that service users are fully aware of the procedure to follow in a case where they feel they have a grievance. Copies of the procedure are contained within WCHP's Operations Manuals held on each WCHP site and are available from staff upon request.

BARRIERS TO CONSULTATION FACED BY CLIENTS

Service user motivation

In contrast to some professionals' perception that clients are not interested in being consulted for strategic planning, the literature and clients involved in this project demonstrated that there are people who want to be involved, and in a way that suits them and meets their needs.

For example, Cummings and his team found that 57 young homeless people in Scotland resented their lack of voice in decision-making and wanted to be consulted about service provision. Care leavers were also very dissatisfied about their involvement and wanted more of a say in their care planning (Cummings, Dickson, Jackson et al. 2000).

Research conducted by the charity Emmaus in 2000, cited in Velasco (2001), found that 80 out of 97 homeless and ex-homeless people wanted to be able to take part in day-to-day decision-making in a shared living scheme.

There may be a concern amongst clients that speaking out might have an adverse effect on how they are treated, and that they might experience pressure or discrimination from the service provider or other clients, although this was harder to evidence. We should be very concerned if these clients are from a hard-to-reach group, e.g. homeless and reliant on a service for shelter and support.

Internally driven barriers

Service users also felt that there were internally driven barriers that prevented them getting involved, as well as barriers presented by service providers:

- fear of looking stupid
- jargon
- inaccessible structures
- lack of feedback
- user involvement used as token gestures or paid lip service.

Personal confidence does have a part to play in motivation, as often clients have expressed the view that they are embarrassed to ask for clarification of jargon or concepts. People who are sleeping rough or have addiction issues may also feel very isolated and stigmatised.

Clients will cease to be motivated to take part in consultation exercises if they do not receive feedback on the action that has been taken as a result of their input. Service users have repeatedly said that there is no point in saying things if no one listens or does anything about it. They have also stated that hearing about a 'no' decision was better than not hearing whether or not a decision had been taken at all.

Black and minority ethnic (BME) groups in Hampshire have reported feeling consultation fatigue as organisations have made many efforts to consult with them, and then not provided any feedback on what (if anything) is to be done as a result.

One service user also pointed out to us that while reimbursing expenses is helpful it is better if these are paid in advance, as often clients do not have the money to cover the costs of attending a meeting or event 'up front'. Reimbursement of expenses is again a professional concept reliant on the fact that staff have access to cash 'up front', either from their own pocket or from a petty cash float.

The ROCC good practice group model

The good practice group in the ROCC research project devised a model of motivation for consultation for their own use, considering themselves as fitting, or having previously fitted, our criteria for hard-to-reach groups.

The model shows a clear awakening to the bigger picture as basic needs are fulfilled, and a client feels more settled. They are then more aware and motivated to participate or be consulted at the higher levels of the former Office of the Deputy Prime Minister (ODPM) once they are out of crisis. There is an interesting parallel with Maslow's hierarchy of needs, where, as needs are fulfilled, individuals move up the eight-stage scale to the highest level. (See p.63 below for an explanation of Maslow's hierarchy of needs.)

As part of the ROCC research project, the good practice group discussed their experiences and feelings about consultation in general, and in particular about strategic planning, and developed a model of motivation to get involved at all (see Box 3.2).

There was usually a trigger for them initially to want to change something in their lives of benefit to them personally, such as giving up crime, or a drug lifestyle. There was then the possibility to seek out someone trustworthy, and preferably someone who had been where the members of the group had been before. This would then reinforce their motivation to change an aspect of their lives and develop an aspiration for a more positive future.

Following the start of a more settled lifestyle, their focus of interest could then widen to a larger community or group, say in a shared house or hostel setting. Positive reinforcement would then enable them to feel able to help others in turn, or contribute more in their defined community and have a sense of belonging. As this sense of belonging grew they would feel more able to champion others or represent their group to a higher authority, and with increased confidence and stability feel a desire to represent others or their group.

Clearly the timescale for this varies in line with an individual's initial motivation and ability to sustain it over time. It also assumes a linear

---

**Box 3.2 Participation in strategic planning –
a process of development and experience**

Describing a personal journey

1. Motivation to change something:

- homelessness

- offending

- drug/alcohol misuse

- chaotic lifestyle.

Focus of interest: individual

2. **Early contact and possibility of change**:

- need for someone who has been through the same experience to understand.

Focus of interest: individual

3. **Early progress**:

- aspirations change, some hope, desire for something better, possibly a tenancy, and/or a more settled life, etc.

Focus of interest: individual and a wider view

4. **Achieving a more settled life**:

- tenancy – awareness of getting and keeping it
- awareness of being part of a local community
- facing up to fear involved in this responsibility and this locality.

Focus of interest: individual and community

5. **Growing confidence to represent myself, other clients, friends, service users**:

- my group or organisation.

Focus of interest: individual as part of a group or organisation.

6. **Member of a group or organisation**:

- Recognition of my group.
- How can my group or organisation represent itself to be seen as important and credible?
- How can our work and worth be recognised?
- Who has the power to help us and how do we talk to them?
- How do we get representation?

Focus of interest: the organisation

7. **My contribution**:

- How can I put something back into the system?
- How can I make a contribution to enable people to benefit from opportunities?
- How can I manage this responsibility?
- What support do I need?

Focus of interest: representative/consultant

development, which the group agreed is not always the case, as there are often self-doubts, or crises of confidence or relapses into old patterns before new, positive ones can be sustained. In addition the vulnerable stage of trusting others can be shortened in the light of new crisis development or unexpected problems occurring.

Here there is a clear awakening to the bigger picture as basic needs are fulfilled, and a client feels more settled. They are then more aware and motivated to participate or be consulted at the higher of the former ODPM levels, again similar to Maslow's hierarchy of needs.

Maslow said that needs must be satisfied in the given order. Aims and drive always shift to next higher order needs. Levels 1 to 4 are deficiency motivators; level 5, and by implication levels 6 to 8, are growth motivators and relatively rarely found. The thwarting of needs is usually a cause of stress, and is particularly so at level 4 (Maslow 1943).

There is evidence that some hard-to-reach individuals have bigger worries than getting involved with strategic planning if their immediate needs are at crisis point. For individuals in longer-term services, there may be a lack of trust that things can change or that they can have a voice, even if they have the inclination.

Box 3.3 A simplified version of Maslow's hierarchy of needs

1. Biological and physiological needs – air, food, drink, shelter, warmth, sex, sleep, etc.

2. Safety needs – protection from elements, security, order, law, limits, stability, etc.

3. Belongingness and love needs – work group, family, affection, relationships, etc.

4. Esteem needs – self-esteem, achievement, mastery, independence, status, dominance, prestige, managerial responsibility, etc.

5. Cognitive needs – knowledge, meaning, etc.

6. Aesthetic needs – appreciation and search for beauty, balance, form, etc.

7. Self-actualisation needs – realising personal potential, self-fulfilment, seeking personal growth and peak experiences.

8. Transcendence needs – helping others to achieve self-actualisation.

Adapted from Maslow (1943)

For women escaping violence, homeless people or those with addiction issues it is likely that at the crisis point they are not often interested in engaging with strategic decision-making processes directly. When the initial crises have passed and they are more settled, then that may well prove to be a more beneficial time to consult with them.

As we have seen, there are barriers faced by service users in some consultation processes offered by supported housing services, and with commissioners of these services. What we have been stressing so far is the need for models and methods to be flexible, combined with a commitment from those in powerful positions to action or enable effective consultation to happen.

One might think that these issues would be less significant for the general population living in the community and wanting to be part of initiatives such as tenants' groups in order to have a voice and a say in aspects of local life that affect them. This, however, is not always the case, and, as we shall see, some structures may benefit from becoming more flexible if a genuine desire is present to seek as wide a representation of view as possible.

The majority of case studies in this book describe how organisations have adopted good practice for service user consultation. The next example, however, shows that there are evident difficulties that provide an interesting challenge. What would you do?

One of the most common complaints concerning the input of tenants' and residents' groups revolves around the level of decision-making entrusted to a small group of individuals whose views are not necessarily representative of the wider communities they are representing. It is a traditional problem, especially where meetings are held during normal daily working hours, effectively denying the vast majority of tenants who work access to the meetings and influence on decisions taken.

Richard Chorley, a freelance writer from Southampton, was on the committee of a tenants' group on a large estate. He believes his experiences are widespread and pose a fundamental challenge to all associations, councils and organisations proposing the inclusion of tenants' groups within serious decision-making processes.

Case study 3.3 Richard's story

To be honest, my experience was quite a disillusioning one. The group would meet on Tuesday or Wednesday afternoons and in the main was attended by single mothers, housewives with young babies and the occasional elderly person. The demographics of the situation were far from inclusive, although this did not seem to bother the representatives from the council's housing and community development teams, who regularly attended the meetings and addressed them on various subjects.

I think the main problem was that there was no chance for working people to attend, as the meetings took place in the middle of the day. This obviously meant the official agents present could place their attendance within their working schedules and their agencies could then subsequently trumpet their supposed policies of inclusiveness as a result.

Given the traditional demographics of the communities concerned, this immediately meant that there was a distinctly low male attendance. All the committee positions were filled by women, as were those of all the visiting agents.

I was quite struck by this and wondered whether the council concerned would have raised an objection had it been a male-dominated environment and committee. I had previously served on the council's race forum and equal opportunities sub-committee, so I was well clued up on the supposed briefs on equalities.

It also shocked me that the group had no constructed advertising policy wherein the majority of tenants could see when and where the group met, and, most importantly, what type of activities and issues it was addressing. The truth was that most residents were unaware of the group's existence, let alone any information as to what type of commitment involvement could demand.

After a while I realised that the threshold of discussion was quite narrow and the gravity of decision-making was restricted to relatively insig-nificant components of estate life. Whilst great play was made about donations of paint for washrooms and playrooms, serious issues that required complex discussion, dissection and analysis were always passed over, sometimes flippantly and seemingly with the support of the officers concerned.

Knowing the area culturally, I soon also realised that the domineering female atmosphere was also likely to alienate certain men from ethnic minorities' communities, and by effect also the women of those communities.

This is all very complex stuff, what I call the 'grey' areas of equality and inclusive culture, and most inclusion policies never really get near to addressing all these refined points.

When I tried to request that meetings were changed to evenings in order to accommodate a more inclusive range of people, the proposal was met with fierce opposition, mainly on the grounds that a lot of the women apparently would not then be able to attend. I have to say I felt there was distinct opposition to the idea of more men joining the committee, even when I pointed out that there were several prominent trade unionists who lived locally who wanted to get involved, and whose experience and knowledge would be invaluable.

Such ideas were blatantly opposed and resulted in an eventual meeting between myself and several housing officers, where a fundamental debate ensued regarding the prime objectives of tenants' committees.

After stating my concerns over the gravity of issues considered, the times of meetings, and the lack of male or ethnic minorities members involved, I was surprised to hear certain perspectives, which, whilst seemingly defending the rights of single mothers or women to attend and take active part, effectively ruled out any realistic chance of most individuals with professional experience of leadership targeting issues and organising serious campaigns or taking a regular part in the tenants groups' decisions or proposals.

I left the group when a council officer told me that 'it was not necessarily about getting the best possible people involved, but maybe some of those who do not normally get involved in anything'. Having studied the constitution of the group, this was in no way defined and the odour of patronising control and retention of power whilst maximising public relations aspects became overpowering, to say the least.

I have since met a number of people from across the country who broadly share the same type of experience, and have voiced their concerns at the motives employed by certain associations and bodies when it comes to tenants' groups.

Experiences of course vary from town to town and region to region, but there does seem to be a case for nationally implemented tenants' groups operational frameworks, constructed to fit the government's own legislation on equal opportunities factors. These could be set up after studying the practices of trade unions, civil rights bodies, religious and cultural sources and other democratic representational bodies' policies regarding operation and the point of maximum inclusion.

Personally, I believe that tenants' groups should be formulated and run in a way that will attract the input of tenants with gifted talents and intellects, who wish to try and represent their community to the best of their abilities, and who will bring a level of valid involvement and knowledge on crucial issues.

This should be done in as broad a sense as possible, but to supposedly grant tenants an inclusive role, whilst designing that structure in a manner that will automatically exclude a large number of those whose lives will be affected by decisions relevant, is not only ineffective, but immoral. This is a crucially important aspect of all strategic planning in the arena and one that demands extremely careful consideration in the next few years.

SUMMARY

There are clear barriers preventing hard-to-reach service users engaging in consultation processes at the strategic level, and, it is fair to say, at any level. Although different groups were faced with different issues, they had some things in common, namely dealing with chaotic lifestyles and difficult problems. These often have the effect of making people feel vulnerable and excluded.

Staff, too, have difficulty sometimes in relinquishing some of the power inherent in their jobs and titles – so you may need to explore the motivation of both staff and service users before any effective work can take place.

Figure 3.1 provides a useful model for discussions. By seeking and acting on service users' views, the service develops and benefits all stakeholders by increasing quality and value.

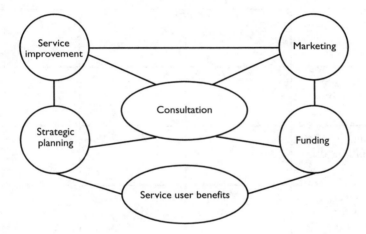

Figure 3.1 The beneficial cycle of service user involvement

Workbook

Using the workbook section of this chapter you can look at barriers that may be present in your workplace, so that they may be overcome, and enable the scene to be set for effective service user consultation.

- What do you feel are barriers to service user consultation?
- Are these greater at the strategic level?
- What are your staff team's barriers?
- Are these greater at the strategic level?

- How will you get over them?
- What are service users' barriers to involvement in consultation?
- How will you help them get over them?
- How will you motivate/train/develop staff and service users?

The table below may help you focus on these areas.

Table 3.1 Motivation and barriers analysis

	Management	*Staff*	*Service users*
Motivation			
Barriers			
How to overcome these			
Development/ training needs			
Your review process for these areas			

CHAPTER 4

Methods that Enable Client Consultation

INTRODUCTION

This chapter reports the views of service users on the different consultation methods used at all levels, including the strategic level. It offers the views of the following service user groups:

- homeless people
- Roma and travellers
- black and minority ethnic (BME)
- people with drug, alcohol and substance issues
- women escaping domestic violence
- young people.

We also include the views of commissioners as well as nine separate, highly practical case studies that you may find useful as inspiration when devising your own strategy.

HOMELESS PEOPLE

Clearly homeless people have more urgent survival needs than strategic planning, but many consultation methods are still valid, and we could improve these methods by enabling greater participation of clients. For example, service users could call their own meetings when they need to, rather than simply attending meetings organised by staff. Another example would be to use these staff-organised meetings as a forum for consulting service users about improvements in services.

Despite the transitory character of the clients using these services, it is still possible to ask their views and collect them over a period of time. For example, it would be possible to ask the same questions of everyone using a service over a year and then collate the results as part of a strategic exercise, to ensure that clients felt that their views counted.

The authors interviewed 68 clients from this group (39 from three day centres and 29 from two direct access hostels in the target region) and found the following:

- Questionnaires worked for this group, as the clients themselves actually saw the results, e.g. in the way day centre space was used.
- Focus groups held at meal times encouraged attendance.
- The healthcare team seeking user evaluation paid participants with a £5 voucher, which was popular.
- The clients thought that newsletters run for users by users were a good idea for sharing views and recommendations for improvement.

These clients also recommended that:

- Organisations should pay service users for giving up their time for consultation and participation work.
- Organisations should consider recruiting and training (and paying) existing service users to become co-consultants, in order to be able to communicate with the hard to reach, in particular those who are street homeless and possibly not accessing any services at all. (Day centres and direct access schemes make more effort to source and provide information about services and options available for the people who use them.)
- Training to use the internet and free access to it within a day centre or direct access scheme might be useful to some of the people who use the schemes.
- Staff teams should hold more regular consultation meetings with service users to talk about things over and above the immediate concerns. This would help service users become accustomed to this type of consultation and ensure that staff feel empowered and able to represent the needs of the people they serve.

ROMA AND TRAVELLERS

Roma and travellers are probably the least popular of all the hard-to-reach groups defined in the introduction. Not only are they homeless, but they are seen as being intentionally so, and rejecting house dwellers' social norms.

Their only media coverage tends to be negative and biased, but they are an ethnic minority group and are entitled to housing-related support services regardless of tenure, along with everyone else who fits the criteria.

We made contact with the Hampshire Gypsy Liaison Officer (GLO), George Summers, and discussed the project with him. He outlined the history of gypsies and travellers, and his role, as well as the legislation that is dealt with regularly. The role of the GLO is to represent gypsies and travellers and act as a go-between in dealing with the council and courts, social services and education authorities, and liaising with any other service that may be needed. George Summers founded the National Association of Gypsy and Traveller Officers and runs training courses twice a year to BTEC standard to enable officers to manage the challenges of the job.

The Caravan Sites Act 1968 made it obligatory for local authorities to provide land sites and management, and 400 were set up across Britain. However, the 1994 Criminal Justice Order Act (Part 5) greatly increased the powers of police and local authorities to evict travellers camping illegally and removed the duty on local authorities, under the 1968 Caravan Sites Act, to provide sites for Roma. It also abolished the government grant available for the construction of Roma caravan sites.

Hampshire's provision for gypsies and travellers is now managed at county level except at a couple of sites that fall under Southampton local authority. Hampshire and the unitary authorities meet quarterly to coordinate a response, but, although it is widely agreed that temporary sites are needed, it is politically unpopular as providing them could cost local members votes. If central government were to re-impose the previous duty, then sites would have to be set up.

The circular produced in February 2006 by the then Office of the Deputy Prime Minister (ODPM), *Planning for Gypsy and Traveller Sites*, recognises the importance of stability for Roma and travellers who wish to purchase their own sites as well as have the right to stop at permanent and temporary sites, and acknowledges that although they only make up 1 per cent of the population, they should still be included in the housing provision planning process. The caravan count in July 2006 noted 16,000 caravans belonging to Roma and travellers around the country, with approximately 75 per cent on permanent sites. Again, this shows a relatively low need but one that has appeared difficult to meet.

This is not just an ethical issue about allowing individuals the right to live in a different way: there is a strong economic argument in terms of the cost of erecting barriers to prevent travellers from using known areas of land, and the cost of eviction in terms of legal fees, and site clearance. In 2002 Bournemouth spent £70,000, and Hampshire in the region of £250,000, on these activities – significantly more than the cost of a field, rubbish collection and water service, which travellers could be charged for.

Although there are 330 permanent sites across the country for 10–30 pitches, there are no transit sites in the whole of the South, Southeast and Southwest. It means that Roma and travellers cannot legally stop for 28 days, as they can in other parts of the country. Those that visit Hampshire have usually got a permanent pitch elsewhere in the country, but move down to the South for work or holidays.

If Roma and travellers do stop somewhere, local protesters usually obtain a court order, effectively ensuring that they will have to move on again within 7–10 days unless there is a reason why they are unable to do so. The GLO makes an assessment to ascertain whether or not there is a genuine need to stay, such as illness, broken vehicles, or a variety of other considerations. The court may grant an eviction order if there is no infringement of the Human Rights Act, so those who do not have an illness or other viable reason to stay have to move on, although this can be challenged if it is felt that the investigation was not thorough enough.

The GLO consulted said that there were some members of these groups who committed crime, and as commercial waste is now taxable this had been a disincentive for them to take rubble or wood to designated dumps. Generally the GLOs' view was that if there were more managed sites these problems could be better handled through dialogue with individuals.

Along with a client living in the rehabilitation stage of a drug and alcohol recovery service who volunteered to help, one of the authors went with Summers to visit two Roma and traveller sites in Hampshire. One site was also attended by the site manager, and the other was a temporary site on public land where the group were hoping to gain the right to remain.

Despite links with local education welfare and health visitors, these individuals are very wary of strangers and Summers explained that anyone interviewed was likely to say what they thought we wanted to hear. He suggested that Roma and travellers would rarely ask for help unless they needed it, for example with reading a letter, as there is a very low level of literacy, owing to the tradition of storytelling to pass on information through generations. (This was now presenting problems for young men having to take the driving theory test as well as the practical driving test.) Also, he said, they were most unlikely to agree to represent others, as they were all aware of their own individual differences within the generic group of Roma and travellers. This was backed up by those we spoke to individually.

None had heard of Supporting People, but understood the concepts of support services. The women said that they liked the health visitor and had

had no difficulties getting children into school, although this was not always the case, and that if they wanted any views to be aired they would tell the GLO about it, as they trusted him. They said that they were not aware of any drug problems amongst their group or others, but that there were sometimes violence and alcohol misuse in their communities, and any difficulties were managed by the group, as outside help was not welcome generally.

Although the Hampshire GLO does have links with education welfare and social services, there were no links with Supporting People. One of the outcomes of the ROCC research project was to remedy this situation, and now the relevant links have been made.

BME GROUPS

The Department of Transport, Local Government and the Regions guide (DTLR 2002) to working with BME groups under Supporting People is a useful starting point for service providers and commissioners, as we need to address other important risks and issues in order to engage and work effectively with these groups.

The first risk relates to labelling and homogenising specific minority ethnic groups, as all too often they are seen as 'the same' – for example, one local authority's well-meaning discussion about having a Black refuge, rather than examining cultural insensitivities and inter-racial discrimination that can lead to exclusion.

Second, there is the risk that individuals from BMEs may also be present in other vulnerable groups receiving housing-related support services as defined in this report.

This brings us to the third risk, that of institutional racism in housing-related support services, or failure to acknowledge the extra dimension of previous or current harassment and discrimination faced by a Black person who is homeless in comparison to a white person who is homeless.

At the risk of generalising, the main view put forward by individuals from BME groups was that they feel marginalised, particularly at the present time, with perceived increasing racism in the UK following '9/11' and the invasion of Iraq. It was also acknowledged that members of these groups often feel 'over-consulted yet under-informed'.

However, progress is being made and Hampshire County Council has commissioned and produced a Race Equality Directory, which identifies over 90 organisations which work with or are run by people from minority ethnic groups. This directory is available on the Hampshire County Council website. (See Useful websites, a section which includes some useful links and websites.)

Community development work project

Hampshire Social Services also commissioned an internal report on the experiences and perceptions of service users from BMEs and the report's recommendations are being implemented. In the pipeline are citizen panels and focus groups as well as what will be called 'retained consultants'. The retained consultants will be paid a fee to respond to any new proposals for council policy and practice, and will be drawn from a range of age groups and backgrounds. They will be paid according to the number of times they respond.

Hampshire County Council also initiated and led a community development work project to build capacity within minority ethnic organisations to enable them to become active participants in planning public services. This project is current and proposals have been made to pool agency resources to provide for the recruitment of three part-time community development workers. By pooling resources it is hoped to make the best and most efficient use of them, ensuring that work is not replicated or confusing to the community through an overload of consultation (which can be the case particularly where minority communities are dispersed and small).

Box 4.1 presents a sample taken from a proposal written by Mohammed Mossadaq, Race Equality Adviser to Hampshire County Council. Consequently two workers were hired and the model proved so successful that another 11 will be in post by April 2008, with a remit for mental health work, part funded by Hampshire Primary Care Trust (PCT).

Southampton City Council Social Cohesion Department produced a three-year plan for their Race Equality Scheme that demonstrates clear open communications with local BME groups. The scheme also acts on the BME groups' wishes – for example, to provide facilities for Muslim burials, following consultation with Muslim faith leaders – and provides funding for an Asian women's refuge. Five per cent of the total revenue grants budget goes to voluntary sector organisations that are led by BME groups or have a direct equality purpose.

It is also important to recognise the mistake of seeing everyone in a particular group as presenting the same issues. For example, there are three established groups of Sikhs in Southampton attending three separate Gurdwara. One group, however, has a high proportion of wealthy landlords, and another has an equally high number of tenants of these landlords – so it cannot be assumed that their needs will all be the same.

Ethnic minorities are significantly under-represented in some key democratic decision-making roles. For example, there are very few school

Box 4.1 Functions of the community development workers

1. to stimulate the development of community activity of minority ethnic groups

2. to expand membership

3. to work with other agencies for joint involvement in community activities

4. to identify possible funding sources.

Management

1. based within the district, preferably at the District Council offices or the Council of Voluntary Services within the geographic area

2. managed by Hampshire County Council with clear links to all the key stakeholders

3. in regular contact with each other to ensure key communication, ideas and best practice is achieved

4. Winchester District Council will hold and manage the pooled funding.

Expectation of achievements

1. longer-term outcomes following the identified need to nurture development. This represents real commitment to the community

2. compliance with statutory requirements by which every agency will be assessed

3. increased participation and integration of minority ethnic communities, a central requirement for sustainable communities.

governors and only one local councillor from ethnic minority communities. Ethnic minorities are not, however, under-represented in the Community Network, a major new partnership in the city. The top priority for the Race Equality Scheme is laying sound foundations to ensure access to culturally sensitive services. This includes improving ethnicity data, identifying and taking action to lift barriers to services, and developing effective monitoring and evaluation processes. The features of the Race Equality Scheme are set out in Box 4.2.

Box 4.2 Southampton City Council BME community consultation and involvement

- [Consultation and involvement is] through an independent monitoring and scrutiny group.

- [Consultation and involvement is] through the development of 'advisory' groups linked to the Monitoring Group whereby people can influence the proposed actions – especially the cross-cutting themes.

- Specific consultation on key actions will also be developed and issues within the scheme will be considered through existing consultation mechanisms.

- This consultation will be specific to the issue under consideration – for example, young people will be asked about youth provision. In this way a range of communities and groups will be engaged using a variety of methods.

- The council's complaints procedure will be amended to enable feedback on race issues to be identified and to influence the development of the scheme if appropriate.

From Race Equality Scheme 2002–2005 *(Southampton City Council 2002)*
The Race Equality Scheme 2002–2005 *has now been replaced by the*
Equality Scheme 2006–2009 *(Southampton City Council 2006)*

The following two case studies look at how one local authority, Southampton City Council, is linking with housing associations in order to consult with BMEs to improve their services. Both are taken directly from the council's public information.

Case study 4.1 Southampton BME Housing Project

In late 2003 the Southampton Housing Partnership successfully applied for a Housing Corporation Community Training and Enabling Grant for a project aimed at increasing awareness of housing options within the BME communities in Southampton.

The partnership acted as the focus for setting up the two-year project and in August 2004 it appointed a project worker to lead the activity.

1. Benefits

The project is focused on delivering the following outcomes:

- the formation of a Southampton BME Housing Steering Group with the skills and resources to develop an evidence-based approach to articulating the housing aspirations of BME communities and the drive to take these forward into workable solutions with the housing partnership and the resources to keep this source of expertise updated

- the production of a Southampton Housing Partnership BME Housing Strategy, which will be integrated into the Housing Strategy by the City Council and the partnership Registered Social Landlords (RSL)

- the development of housing-focused community networks that will enable all RSLs in the city to better implement good practice in respect of Race Equality and Diversity

- increased knowledge and understanding among the BME community of the work of the five partner RSLs in the city

- a greater understanding by the partner housing associations of the ways in which they can implement the Race Equality Code of Practice for Housing Associations (Race and Housing Inquiry Panel 2002) and Section 2.7 of the Housing Corporation's Regulatory Code and Guidance (Housing Corporation 2005).

2. Links with other organisations

The Southampton Housing Partnership, which founded the BME Partnership, consisted of First Wessex Housing Group (HG), Hyde Housing Association, Oriel HG, Raglan Housing Association, Western Challenge Housing Association and Southampton City Council. In April 2007 a new partnership was commissioned, bringing the following organisations together – First Wessex HG, Hyde HA, Swaythling HS, Western Challenge HA, Hermitage HA, Testway HA, Sovereign HA and Southampton CC. The example of the Southampton BME Housing Project was related to the authors in a telephone conversation with Don John, then Equalities and Diversity Officer for Southampton City Council.

The second case study follows how one of these housing associations is working to liaise better with local BME service users within their sheltered housing schemes.

Case study 4.2 Understanding each other – developing links with BME community groups (Western Challenge Housing Association)

All sheltered housing staff have an objective to develop links with BME community groups. To assist this, we developed a toolkit and launched this at a conference together with presentations from three members of the supported housing team. We have achieved the following:

- We made links with Southampton Voluntary Services, who have links with many community groups, and we are able to access their database.

- A BME speaker from Roshini Day Centre has given a talk to East team re connecting with BME groups.

- We have made links with Southampton Social Services to link up with the cultural centre operating on our doorstep in Bugle Street.

- We are planning visits to see centres of worship so that scheme managers are familiar with other religious groups and promote Western Challenge Hosuing Association and our schemes.

- We gave a talk to the Residents' Association at their AGM in Upper Bugle Street to get feedback on the possibility of a cultural event. We are now consulting residents at all our sheltered schemes in Southampton to see how many tenants would want this and also to get costing.

- We have approached an Asian drama group to give us a proposal. The purpose of this event would be to involve residents, link with community groups, and raise awareness for staff and tenants and invite key stakeholders.

- In the Christchurch area, we are making links with Chinese/Jewish groups and finding out what groups exist in the Bournemouth area.

Other links with the community

The team have successfully developed links in the Ringwood and Fordingbridge areas and invited local residents to social events. One of the actions that will come from the Best Value review of these schemes will be to investigate the possibility of setting up a resource centre at Quaker Court. We have a high dependency group here and feel that residents would benefit from other professional agencies being able to work alongside us at the scheme.

We will also be seeking to remodel the service at our specialised sheltered schemes to meet some of the domestic needs of tenants that can be funded through Supporting People.

Other improvements

The introduction of support planning is the most significant improvement that we are currently working on. This has already brought benefits for tenants. One example was a tenant at Barnstaple who had asked to transfer because she was finding difficulty climbing stairs to her first floor flat. In the Southampton Housing Officer's (SHO) assessment, she expressed a desire to stay where she was – this has now been achieved through a second handrail.

Another example was a tenant at a specialised sheltered scheme who did not join in social activities. When this was explored as part of the assessment it transpired that it was because she had a hearing aid, which is a problem in a communal setting. We are now pursuing the installation of loop systems in all our sheltered schemes. It is early days as we have only undertaken 12 assessments as part of the pilot but anticipate that support planning will bring real benefits in meeting tenants' needs and enabling them to retain their independence in the community.

Where appropriate, joined-up consultation is a priority action and will take place with the police and the PCT. There is no reason why these groups could not make links with Supporting People and consultation take place within networks currently in development, to avoid replication, as the broader issue for this group is one of inclusion.

Other methods used are community outreach teams that work with both established groups and newer groups such as asylum seekers, to help meet their needs and take on their views in shaping service delivery. For example, the Youth Service are in the process of developing different focus groups such as Bengali girls and Somali boys, so that the service can ask different gender and ethnic groups about the service they receive, what they are currently getting, and what they think their needs and wants are.

Key messages

It is acknowledged that social care services often fail to recognise the additional needs presented by someone from an ethnic minority on top of the presented problem – for instance, on top of being homeless. Part of engaging with individuals from BME groups is recognising the individuals' needs (rather than making assumptions about groups), as well as the issues of dis-crimination and harassment that they face on a regular basis.

Portsmouth City Council has operated a multicultural link group for nine years now, but has only recently launched the group officially. Membership is drawn from anyone who has a role in working with or having a responsibility for BMEs in the voluntary and statutory sectors, as well as the community at large. All the prevalent ethnic minorities are represented and the smaller or newer ones encouraged to attend.

Three years ago the city council held a one-day conference for BMEs that was sensitive to cultural needs and with mother-tongue speakers, in order to seek their views on statutory provision such as health and social services. Over 100 people participated and the views were collated and passed on to the relevant departments. In 2001–02 a 'valuing diversity' survey was conducted in partnership with MORI, and 777 questionnaires were completed.

Recently the Portsmouth Racial Equality Network Organisation was set up as a purely consultative body and provided with a timetable of issues, policies, etc. that members are to be consulted on over the coming year. Membership is drawn from those individuals with dual language skills (often younger people), who have access to greater numbers of people in their communities, as opposed to the traditional community leaders of BME groups. The organisation held a conference to which all the member groups were invited. They consulted with the groups about how effectively they felt communicated with and informed about services by statutory service providers such as health and housing departments.

It is clear that there are effective networks in operation for BME groups in Hampshire, Portsmouth and Southampton, and that Supporting People could make use of these when they wish to consult on strategic issues as part of a wider and more inclusive process.

The continued training of professionals (including perhaps service providers and also commissioners) in valuing diversity, genuine equality of opportunity and anti-discriminatory practice would help to raise awareness of the issues facing individuals from BME groups, who need inclusion in the wider community with improved access to housing-related support services.

PEOPLE WITH DRUG, ALCOHOL AND SUBSTANCE ISSUES

This section reports the findings from 32 clients from four agencies providing detoxification, rehabilitation and support group services.

Clients said that due to the nature of the residential units there is a high expectation of compliance to a set regime, so they would not expect to be consulted much about service changes. They did, however, feel that:

- group meetings were useful in sorting out day-to-day issues and some service level arrangements
- the most valuable and effective consultation method was discussion with their keyworker on a one-to-one basis

- generally they were informed about what was available to them prior to coming to services but very unaware of housing options available to them, which generated a high level of anxiety amongst those due to move on.

The findings further showed that:

- 60 per cent were interested in being consulted at a strategic level for Supporting People, as they felt that housing-related support services and housing were critical issues for their future successes
- 80 per cent were very interested in meeting with commissioners to convey their views
- 20 per cent felt that they might like training in the nature of strategic planning and decision-making, and expressed a need to be taken seriously and not patronised.

In the view of the consultant, 'the majority of the service users...were both capable and keen to advocate for themselves and whilst they might appreciate staff support they did not necessarily need it' (Marc Mordey). This may have been due to the therapeutic and constructively confrontational models of treatment often used in drug rehabilitation schemes, which often lead to significantly increased skills.

Overall, as with homeless service users, those not yet resettled were more concerned with their immediate housing needs than those who had moved on, and were interested in being consulted at a strategic level, although less than 5 per cent of this group expressed any desire to be paid to do so.

The recommendations from these clients are as follows.

1. Supported housing providers/Supporting People teams need to provide much more information about what is available in the supported housing sector to service users.

2. Information could be carried in places like libraries, in *The Big Issue*, in flyers and through leaflets and other printed matter left at drop-in centres and other places service users visit.

3. Information should be designed, using service users as the consultants, to ensure that it is the information that people actually need and want.

4. Commissioners should be prepared to spend time visiting service users 'on site' and need to do so on a regular basis to ensure ongoing contact and liaison. Service users should always be consulted as to whether they would rather meet commissioners individually or as a group.

5. Housing associations, local authorities and other support agencies should come and visit substance misuse services and their users on a regular basis – with 'roadshows', possibly videos, and the opportunity to meet with their own service users too.

6. Local authorities should be prepared to explain the points system[1] to service users in a way that makes sense to them.

Case study 4.3 shows how service delivery was changed in line with service users' needs and wishes in a substance and alcohol service for women.

Case study 4.3 Brighton Oasis Project

The service set up a forum for service users – this was initially staff-led and had few attendees.

Over time staff have attended training on client empowerment and the forum has become more focused on the issues women want to discuss, and the service users have devised the terms of reference to ensure that they benefit from attending meetings. The forum democratically elects a chair who holds fortnightly surgeries and then takes forward the views of the forum by having a place on the trustees board. The board has agreed to accept whoever is voted on by the forum, providing that the voting has been conducted fairly.

In order for this to happen a lot of work went into inducting the chair about the board, budgets, strategic planning, etc., and the client representative is able to use the chair of the board as a mentor between meetings. Meetings have in turn had to become jargon-free and more interesting, which has benefited all members.

In this way, the service users' forum has a clear and workable link with the board, who in turn link in with local commissioners. One local commissioner did offer vouchers for women to attend a large consultation meeting at a local centre, but they did not wish to attend such a large-scale event, so he has been asked to visit the service users within the forum setting to let him know their views.

There have been many positive outcomes of having user representation on the board. Service users have influenced publicity materials and the design of services within the project, and have made a two-tier system into a flexible package tailored to the needs of the individuals, so a combination

---

1   Local authority housing is allocated on a points system. Points are given in order to prioritise access to this limited resource – for example, points are given for people with a local connection, poor health and disability, etc.

of the staged programme and drop-in support is now available. Crucially, we have always provided childcare, so that women can take the time they need to benefit fully from the services they receive.

More recently, forum members applied for funding under the Drugscope Millennium Award and were awarded £15,000 to spend on activities that would benefit them and also the local community. They are taking part in creative writing, photography and craft projects, with a planned end result of a 40-page magazine resource.

Our next example looks at how women with previous drug, alcohol or substance misuse issues worked together to set up an information service that would be of benefit to other women in the region. Here we see that solid organisation and networks with other service users groups have contributed to the success of the project.

Case study 4.4 Kernow Women in Touch (KWIT)
Overview

The 'Kernow Women in Touch' (KWIT) project started in 2003 and originated through the thoughts and shared life skills of four women living in the area. In a bid to try and provide an improved level on information and advice for local women, the group's first concerted project as an organisation was the research and publication of a handbag-sized leaflet on all services available to women in the Cornwall region. In their second year the group's application for Drug and Alcohol Action Team (DAAT) funding was successful, and included provision of a seven hours' weekly payment for a coordinator.

The funding was given in acknowledgement of the huge amounts of work and dedication needed in order to get service users together, without a perpetual network of contacts being activated literally every day of the week!

In a rural area, mailshots and phone contact are essential and there is also the issue of travel costs. Reimbursing these costs encourages subsequent attendance and support for the programmes, thus leading to genuine growth and potential expansion for the future.

Having recognised the need for tight administration and effective communication channels, KWIT was pleased to accept umbrella support from a local day planning agency. This relationship gave the group access to computers and premises in addition to invaluable consultation for the coordinator, within the arenas of information and staff welfare. The determination to be all-inclusive soon led KWIT to realise that mailing merely from agency data stores was not going to be sufficient in terms of reaching maximum potential service users. As such, an ongoing research element revolves around attempting to answer that question.

Reaching user groups

A committee of members sufficiently involved in recovery and dedicated to building 'routes' to user groups has been set up and is expanding as enthusiasm for the programme grows. Members of the committee share life skills and their time and commitment to an idea that has grown from the simple vision of four local women, determined to do something to improve the quality of life experienced by the people of Cornwall.

Currently the committee reaches user groups via various routes including:

- networking input from professional committee members within their fields of work and expertise

- members' attendance of Alcoholics Anonymous and Narcotics Anonymous meetings

- links and liaisons with other agencies such as Domestic Violence Forum, higher education channels, family and carer groups, National Treatment Agency (NTA), GPs and other relevant agencies.

The group also publishes a monthly newsletter that goes to all user groups and members, and publicises dates of events and programmes. This communication also allows for feedback from groups and individuals regarding new and established programmes. The newsletter includes transport provision details to ensure that service users have the maximum incentive to attend events.

As part of her formal remit, the coordinator attends the local Implementation Planning Group's committee meetings and stages presentations at a number of prominent seminars and conferences in the region.

There is an annual Cornish DAAT 'Getting Better' conference, and KWIT is now playing a large role in the promotion and publicity surrounding this event.

As well as these formal environments, the group organises a wide social programme with visits to beaches, local attractions, shopping centres and the theatre, which have proved extremely popular with service users. The social element is crucially important because it helps to ensure that service users regain a sense of normality and an improved quality of life in recovery and into the future.

At the KWIT meetings there are often guest speakers covering a host of topics. These range from general health issues, services, detox theory and availability, political and planning matters, all the way to body massage and facials!

Two-way feedback discussion follows these meetings, with points of interest and importance being relayed back out in information to members, conferences and meetings.

Achievements

An idea of KWIT's impact in Cornwall can be gleaned from the fact that the group's coordinator has been elected onto the National Users' Advisory Forum in London. This follows invaluable input from two KWIT members on the South West User Forum, which provides direct feedback into strategic planning of services and treatment. The position on a nationally recognised committee provides serious credibility for KWIT, who also benefit considerably from the vital information disclosed in national-level discussion and planning.

Ultimately KWIT measures its impact so far by the impressive number of member service users who have joined the group in its first two years. The group is also proud of the high level of posted feedback it receives from user groups – this is an aspect of KWIT's success that is quite rare in this sector.

While its member and committee bases have gone from strength to strength, the group feels that a collective sense of commitment, purpose and vision is increasing simultaneously. Increased response levels from other agencies and a willingness to refer to an organisation are always a sure-fire means of assessing its impact and profile, and KWIT has experienced a massively significant rise in these interactive areas of operation.

Plans for the future

Immediate plans for future programmes include bidding for funding for a Cornwall service users' forum, a men's support group, based on the experience and success of the women's programmes, and strategic planning for the future establishment of a daily drop-in centre.

KWIT is heavily active in mentoring and is currently providing peer support for the region's new post-detox four-week programme. This input has arisen as a direct result of service user consultation, and subsequent user demand that other agencies include KWIT in the planning and delivery of service programmes.

KWIT believes that proper organisation over a suitable period of time is the most important element required in order to maximise service user participation and creative input. The group has built on a dedicated, central core of members whose passionate commitment and stamina have ensured that there is a solid base from which the group can now advance and expand. Local training courses are being constructed currently, to serve as induction platforms for service users, wherein they will learn how KWIT fits in alongside DAATs, the NTA, PCTs, and about the roles that presentations, public speaking, administration, technology and advocacy play in the group's overall work.

As the group advances individually, both committee and members are united in the belief that further cooperation and referral work with other service user groups is the way forward within the service provision industry. It will be this fundamental principal that firmly underpins the exciting expansions and challenges that KWIT intends to meet during the foreseeable future.

WOMEN ESCAPING DOMESTIC VIOLENCE

This section is based on the findings from 23 women at five refuges in the target area.

As for other homeless people, living in shared temporary accommodation and trying to get rehoused can often be a stressful experience. Women in refuges often have the responsibility of children in tow, and have recently fled an abusive partner, so have a lot of immediate needs to attend to. Consequently these individuals do not have a great interest in looking at strategic issues at this early stage. Women who have moved through the system and are now ready to move on, or have already done so, are interested in participating in consultation and planning of services, as they see themselves as having a clear understanding of the particular needs of this group.

It was clear from the fieldwork that the relationship with the staff is of great importance for women in refuges, and they rely on them for support and information. Generally the refuge system has encouraged an ethos of empowering vulnerable women escaping abuse as a method of rebuilding their self-esteem and confidence shattered by an abusive partner. Many women were anxious to maintain their anonymity if they were to attend external meetings, in view of the risk of being seen by the partner they were fleeing and having their names on documents, etc.

Key findings

- 90 per cent of the women interviewed said that they were consulted about the everyday running of the service and felt that they were listened to, as evidenced by changes made where it was possible to resource them in the refuge services.

- Useful methods include: noticeboards, house meetings and support meetings, as well as the one-to-one discussions women had with their keyworkers.

- 90 per cent of women felt strongly that they would like commissioners to come and see them in the refuge, as they felt more secure there and it would give commissioners an insight into how they lived.

- 80 per cent of women were not interested in participating in management meetings, and also felt some doubt about the ability of one client to present potentially diverse views on their behalf.

- Two women who expressed an interest thought that they could only be involved once they were living in their new accommodation.

- 80 per cent of women felt happy about staff representing their views at management and other external meetings, as they regularly received feedback on progress.

- 85 per cent did not want a generic 'user group', preferring the idea of sharing information with other women who had been in situations similar to themselves.

- 15 per cent were keen to see an independent group set up with the purpose of being consulted as part of strategic planning, as well as having an advocacy and campaigning role.

- 80 per cent of women interviewed would like to be more involved in decision-making at all levels.

- The women were interested in all the following proposed formats: peer/buddy systems, creative writing and websites.

- 75 per cent of women were interested in a website where they could exchange information and share views, although they raised concerns about system security breaches and safety for themselves and their children in using 'chatrooms'. (NB The Refuge charity website has a large button that enables site visitors to hide their visits.)

Generally, women were cynical about their influence with funders, based on their previous experiences, and felt that, although staff could represent their views, 'response to their needs was limited'.

Good practice example

In one refuge some women from the support group, who were ex-residents but continuing to use support services, had become more involved in consultation at strategic level.

A successful example of consultation at a strategic level was one refuge's involvement in developing a local domestic violence strategy. Initially local authority officers (both women) visited the refuge to consult women, and invited them to feed their views into the strategy. Women and children in the refuge wrote about their experiences, and one woman accompanied staff to Domestic Violence Forum meetings to read out service users' writings, and represent their views.

The women concerned felt the success of this was due to two main things:

- the approach taken by the local authority officers – who were prepared to come to them, had positive attitudes, were very encouraging and led the women to believe that their views were important and would have impact
- the support that staff provided through discussions, writing, and particularly by helping the women to develop the confidence to attend the meetings and speak out.

Twenty-five per cent of the women we interviewed would be happy to go to external meetings provided that:

- the meetings had a clear purpose and were preferably time-limited rather than ongoing
- transport was provided or paid for if the venue was difficult for access
- meetings were held in school hours and childcare was provided for smaller children.

Women with young children would be unable to attend without this, and many women in refuges do have young families.

We have included the next example (Case study 4.5) because criticism has been levied at the Sure Start initiative, but here we have found an example of the system working well and with active involvement and consultation of service users at the top.

Case study 4.5 Weston Sure Start

Sure Start local programmes are a government initiative to meet the needs of babies and children up to five years old, in terms of health, education and social welfare. The original schemes were set up in areas of high depriva- tion with a view to benefiting the immediate local community.

In Weston, Southampton, Sure Start is next door to Weston Shore Infants School and runs a variety of activities for parents and children living in the area. New parents and families moving into local authority accom- modation are contacted and given the opportunity to register with Sure Start and so benefit from a range of local facilities.

Although accountability for the programme lies with the local authority, the priorities and local direction are determined by the parents and agency Forum.

Many of the parents who use the service often lack confidence, are lonely and have low self-esteem initially, but soon develop confidence in their abilities to contribute at a strategic level, deciding on resource allocation and service development in a mutually supportive and egalitarian environment.

One recent initiative suggested by parents has been work with the Fire Service who have offered fire training and prevention. The area has experienced an unusually high level of callouts which have significantly reduced since the input from the Fire Service.

Another area of concern raised by parents is that male single parents may feel excluded in a predominantly female environment, so, in consultation with fathers, efforts have been made to have more family-based activities in preference to special sessions for men, as they did not want them.

This is an excellent example of how empowering service users can lead to useful and popular developments, rather than providing services that users do not want – which can often happen when services do not ask what the clients want.

YOUNG PEOPLE

This section looks at a diverse and ever-increasing group of service users: young people. Chapter 6 in this book is dedicated to the Young Men's Christian Association (a specialist service for young people), and here we have chosen to highlight other services applying young people's views in a creative and accessible manner. Young people can be challenging and energetic and have been seen time and again to want to stretch and grow in more creative directions than some of our 'older' client groups.

Who are 'hard-to-reach' young people?

Obviously not all young people are vulnerable by definition, but this study was interested in young people who may be hard to reach for the following reasons:

- homeless
- drug and/or alcohol issues
- involved in or at risk of offending
- in care or care leavers
- aged 16–21 for the purposes of Supporting People.

We interviewed some young people in the fieldwork for homeless people and drugs/alcohol misuse, and they were amongst the keenest to be involved in strategic decision-making for Supporting People.

Our focus was, however, on those young people already involved in consultation for strategic decision-making, as this already appeared to be happening in Hampshire. We felt this was a good opportunity to find out how young participants felt the systems were working, in particular through the Care Action Team, the Hampshire Young Pregnancy Strategy group, the Youth Council and Connexions. We also included two young women whom we had interviewed in our discussions with members of a Roma and travellers' group.

Connexions

Connexions, the national service for linking all young people aged 13–19 years in to information systems, has been in Hampshire since September 2002 and currently has 67 staff. There are pilot district one-stop shop schemes in Gosport, Winchester and Fareham, whose function is to promote information that can be of use to young local people. These have been planned in terms of where young people go and how they can have their say, so, for example, in rural areas such as villages, signposts have been used to advertise services and information.

There are also links to schools and the youth service at district and county levels and young people are being hired as mentors and representatives at all levels. On the Isle of Wight and in Hampshire young people were thoroughly enjoying their role, as they saw it as an exciting and challenging job to support other young people, and also have a voice at a high level.

Across all these services young people said that their motivation was primarily to help other young people of the future who may have had similar or worse life experiences, and to increase their own skills personally and professionally. It was also important that their work commitment was flexible, to fit in with benefit or other job/training requirements.

Here are some examples that the young people we interviewed identified as good practice.

Good practice example 1: Care Action Team

Through Connexions and the young people in our good practice group and particularly in the Isle of Wight, we hope to find out the views of young people on how they would want to be involved in strategic decision-making. We have seen good practice represented through the Care Leavers' Panel designed by Morag Currie at Hampshire Social Services.

A multi-agency panel will consider each care leaver's need for housing and housing support and work together to provide it. By using a new database of its social housing, Hampshire has managed to identify gaps across its 11 district councils. This should prevent young people becoming homeless and help them to live independently and successfully and not let them fall through the net. Morag regularly consults with the Care Action Team, a group of young people who mentor other young people and contribute to strategic planning through consultation processes such as a housing workshop.

One issue facing young people is that of teenage pregnancy, and for some this results in leaving home voluntarily or otherwise, leaving the young parent vulnerable and potentially homeless or in need of housing-related support. In this context a good example of service user involvement at the strategic level is the Hampshire Teenage Pregnancy Strategy Planning Group, who have an annual conference involving relevant organisations and young people, including teenage parents.

Good practice example 2: Teenage Pregnancy Strategy Planning Group Conference

This conference held on 30 June 2003 was a full day at which the 'chair' presented the background to the strategy for Hampshire, service users offered their experiences and views for service development, and all participants offered amendments to be considered at the September meeting of the group.

The three teenage mothers spoke clearly and eloquently on their experiences, both good and bad, and highlighted the importance of being able to continue education while still of school and college age, and of adequate housing with support to manage their pregnancies and early years' childcare.

Other young people, namely Ashley, Emily and Emma, were also there from the Care Action Team and Connexions and contributed fully to the events. They gave their views on meaningful and effective methods of consulting with young people. (Top tips: provide food and transport!) They also talked in depth about what motivated them to support other young people, and this was basically being able to make a difference, even if it was only a small change, to another young person's life, in a very similar vein to adults entering social care as a profession.

Ashley said they all held a strong belief in integrating services for young people so that these were more accessible, and that information could be shared more effectively and appropriately between agencies. Ashley felt that a lot of assumptions were still made about what is good for young people instead of asking for their opinions, and if relevant facts are presented young people can make their own decisions about the course of their lives. Ashley said that adults could not represent young people adequately without genuine consultation and that needs should be assessed individually, as not all young people are the same.

The young people the authors spoke to also felt that commissioners should ask young people about their views. The commissioners could take time out to visit them in places where young people congregate, e.g. youth groups, Connexions, youth councils, etc.

Ashley said that, as well as being vice chair for the Hampshire County Youth Council, he was also a member of the Children and Young People's Unit – a national forum for young people that discusses issues affecting young people and speaks to government ministers directly. This is similar to the UK Youth parliament, where young people are elected in similar ways to the national parliament and have select committees with specific focuses, which Emma is involved in. Ashley is also involved in a variety of other groups, such as the Youth Health Council.

Good practice example 3: Changes! Southern Ltd.

Changes! is a social enterprise offering a unique service to looked after children, working in Portsmouth and South East Hampshire.

Changes!
Southern limited

Improving the lives of Looked After Children

Figure 4.2 Changes! Southern Ltd. logo

Changes! provides the following services:

- Care Changes – Changes! facilitates an involvement project for young people in local authority care. A group of young people meet weekly to discuss issues, support each other, and seek to represent the views of 'looked after' children to social services authorities and associated agencies who are directly involved with children and young people who are in, or have been in, the care system in shaping relevant policies and services in the city.

- Mentoring – structured one-to-one support is provided for vulnerable young people to divert them from a negative lifestyle and promote social inclusion. It also aims to improve every aspect of their lives, including emotional and physical health and increase education and training opportunities.

- Current service priorities are to work with young people who are experiencing or at risk of social exclusion, and to focus on all aspects of their lives according to the Green Paper 'Every Child Matters' (DfES 2003).

- Changes! promotes and supports opportunities for looked after children to access education and training, adapt a healthy lifestyle, and increase social skills.

- Changes! provides training for young people to encourage confidence and positive self-esteem, in order to become young leaders in the projects they are involved in and to eventually seek the opportunity to become a volunteer registered with millennium volunteers. The opportunities are in activities such as weekly gym sessions, consultation work, and social activities such as snooker and cinema and summer programmes and eventually lead on to peer mentoring.

Involvement of young people

All looked after children and care leavers referred to Changes! are vulnerable for one reason or another. This may be as a result of family breakdown, problems at school or involvement in criminal activities.

Changes! works with young people at risk and enables them to access a variety of projects under the Changes! umbrella. These include community-based diversion activities such as gym sessions, school holiday activity schemes and participation in local and regional consultations. We also deliver more intensive work using one-to-one support and group-based learning programmes, such as life skills and the young leader progression programme – which provides a vehicle for young people to have set goals in place to focus on personal development and put something back into their community.

Changes! currently employs paid staff working on the different projects, but also recruits, trains and supports sessional workers and volunteers on an ongoing basis, who receive relevant training according to their post; many of them support individual referrals. Changes! actively promotes consultation with young people to support the development of new and existing services, and through doing so enables them to participate in wider consultation exercises. This is a rare opportunity for excluded and vulnerable young people to have their say but also develop real citizenship skills in negotiation, public speaking and assertion.

Young people who access Changes! projects have opportunities to develop:

- relationship-building skills
- self-esteem and self confidence
- clear and consistent boundaries of behaviour
- more positive attitudes about themselves and others
- personal self-care skills including sexual health
- communication skills
- support with access to employment, training and education
- social network development.

Changes! staff actively work with external agencies to support young people, often advocating on their behalf, attending inter-agency planning meetings and reviews, and introducing young people to constructive social activities and specialist support services.

Care Changes!

This project is supported by Portsmouth Social Services Department and delivered by Changes! to provide a voice for young people who are or who have been in local authority care. The project has been involved in a wide range of consultations both locally and nationally. In the past, these have included:

- 'Every Child Matters' – Green Paper
- Food Standards for Looked After Children
- National Healthy Care Standards
- Home Office Drug Strategy
- University of Portsmouth Service Users Group
- Portsmouth Children and Adolescent Mental Health Strategy.

Young people from the Care Changes! project have also been involved in foster carer training, interviews for social services staff, and training for student social workers, in the process of interviewing, assessing and guest lecturing level 1, 2 and 3 of the social work degree.

In February 2004, ten young people participated in Total Respect training. This was commissioned by Portsmouth City Council and delivered by the National Youth Advocacy Service.

The training was for councillors and senior managers through to front-line practitioners, mostly from social services, and focused on how young people can be listened to and their views genuinely heard. The young people have also been involved in an ongoing way with the National Healthy Care Standards consultation in Portsmouth, and as a direct result of their input in both these forums three major changes have been achieved in 2004:

1. The local authority does not give black bin liners to young people when they move. As a demonstration of respect, the local authority will provide a bag or suitcase of the young person's choice when they move. As far as we are aware, Portsmouth is the first local authority in the country to have made this change from February 2004.

2. When looked after young people want to sleep over at a friend's house, the friend's parents will no longer need to be checked by the police.

3. To help support placement moves, social services have created a young person's 'passport' – this is a personal portfolio of information a young person would like to exchange with the carer prior to the placement. This includes likes and dislikes about food, interests, and other information to help break the ice and help young people and carers get to know each other.

Feedback is regularly gathered through reviews where young people are encouraged to comment on the support they have received.

Changes! has a monitoring, recording and evaluation system in place to ensure best outcomes for all young people we work with.

Box 4.3 What young people say about Changes!

'They has a laugh and help you when you need them.'

'I think it (mentoring) has helped me to be more confident, stay out of trouble and understand more things.'

'They helped me a lot through bad times and some behaviour problems.'

'Without workers believing me I would not be where I am now.'

Case study 4.6 Creative consultation

Cube Consulting was asked to seek the views of all young people on living in the London Borough of Tower Hamlets. The borough has one of the youngest populations in the country, so the local authority wanted to ensure that the voice of all young people, especially vulnerable young people, was heard and responded to.

Cube Consulting's consultancy methodologies were varied in order to ensure accessibility to all young people, and include the following.

Young people's focus group

Cube Consulting set up a small young people's focus group to take a lead on the consultation programme and to advise Cube Consulting on the content of the questionnaire and the methodologies adopted.

Questionnaire

Cube Consulting designed a questionnaire and sent this to all young people in schools and youth clubs, with the incentive of prizes for individual responders and their school or club. It placed a full-page advertisement in the local press to advertise the questionnaire, which could also be downloaded on the dedicated website created for the young people of Tower Hamlets (www.amp.uk.net). Consultants also went into schools and clubs to promote the questionnaire and encourage young people to respond by completing the simple form.

Actors

Cube Consulting worked with professional actors to deliver role-plays and discussion sessions in primary and secondary schools and in youth clubs to gain initial views of young people. The actors then went to a larger number of schools a month later to test the key themes that were being expressed by delivering creative workshops. The workshops included more role-plays, debates, artwork and poetry writing. This proved to be a very accessible way of encouraging young people to express their views on what life was like living in Tower Hamlets.

Workshops

Trained facilitators went into secondary schools and clubs to deliver workshops during citizenship lessons to encourage discussion and elicit views from all students. There were lively debates and key issues were expressed.

Outcomes

Cube Consulting reported the findings back to the young people's focus group and an inter-agency group of professionals who worked with young people. As a result, a Young People's Plan was produced, which provides the strategic driver for joined-up services for young people throughout the borough. Cube Consulting also developed a borough-wide youth participation strategy to ensure that service providers would continue to hear and act upon the views of young people.

Case Study 4.7 Winchester College: young people and creative method

Students on a drama and video degree course at Winchester College have been working on a community-based project in partnership with City Road, a hostel for care leavers run by Winchester Care and Support.

The students sought the manager's consent and advertised the project on the hostel noticeboard. Young people then expressed an interest in being part of a drama and video project.

The students turned up weekly for three hours at a time in the evening over three months. Their aim was to help young people express themselves through the media of video and drama, provide them with an interesting and potentially therapeutic activity, and increase their video-making skills. The end product was a film to be shown at an 'in-context viewing' (an art installation) at the King Alfred's College, to which young people and service providers were invited.

The students said they believed young people had benefited from being able to express their views about their lives in the hostel, including their likes and dislikes. The students also perceived that the young people were interested in learning new skills, as well as feeling they could connect with the students, who were also young people with a lot of similarities. For example, both groups share issues such as living in shared accommodation, managing independent living and having little available cash. Young people have also said they feel that the students can understand them, that they care, and that the project has been a positive diversion from less healthy activities.

An in-context viewing was later held at King Alfred's College, and, by taking their shoes off on arrival, participants at the viewing were invited to be without their usual footwear and follow in the 'paper footsteps' of a young care leaver using the service. A realistic mock-up of a young care leaver's bedroom was complete down to the unfinished take-away and person asleep in bed!

Although the project was not designed with service review in mind, and the user involvement project is aimed at strategic involvement, there were useful links to be made. Service users' views and issues about the care system were evident throughout the presentation, and did make a contribution to strategic decision-making by the chief executive and commissioners for young peoples' services.

COMMISSIONERS' VIEWS

Although the focus of the ROCC project was on how hard-to-reach clients wanted to be consulted about strategic planning for Supporting People, the team decided that we should also seek commissioners' views. We wanted to identify the value the commissioners placed on clients' views, how much these were weighted against other considerations, methods they currently use or would be happy to use, and how they thought about reaching the 'hard to reach'.

The team also considered it was useful to seek the commissioners' views on the nature of representation and how highly they rated consultation gained independently from providers as part of a planning cycle.

There was very little consensus on what commissioners deemed hard-to-reach clients, and some said that they were not even getting to the 'easy to reach'. The commissioners felt a better description would be that clients were hard to engage with rather than to reach, and they cited, for example, older people in care homes as 'easy to reach, but hard to engage, as they just wanted things to stay the same'.

This in itself does not demonstrate that the older people are necessarily hard to engage, but suggests that they may be of a generation that was taught not to complain, or perhaps the methods for consulting them are not sufficient to engage them fully. Some commissioners also stated that commissioners themselves should be easier to reach, rather than clients being seen as hard to reach. A few commissioners felt that some clients could not engage in consultation exercises as they did not have the health or mental capacity. Almost all those interviewed felt that few clients would be interested in strategic planning, especially if they were in our defined hard-to-reach group, and that this interest would only be apparent where they had received validation of involvement in their support plans and daily activities.

The commissioners also stated on several occasions that even within a group not all individuals necessarily participate in discussions, through either self-exclusion, apathy or lack of confidence, or for other reasons. However, skilled facilitation can determine whether or not silence means assent or dissent, or finding out whether a group is the best method of communicating with these individuals.

CURRENT SERVICE USER INVOLVEMENT ACROSS THE DIFFERENT SUPPORTING PEOPLE PARTNERS IN HAMPSHIRE

Current involvement differs, in the authors' region, across the main Supporting People partners – health, probation, social services and Youth Offending Teams.

Health organisations appeared to be both more committed to, and actually practising, direct involvement in both the development of strategic objectives and actual services. This seems to reflect both the youth of the structures and the possibly related ability to assign significant resources to user involvement.

Probation personnel whom we interviewed seemed to have little or no commitment to user involvement in any form, perhaps reflecting the service's tight focus on a small number of key, central government-imposed targets.

The approach of the local authorities varied according to their context (unitary or two-tier) and internal culture. Some seemed very committed to involving user groups and were actively setting up mechanisms to do this – usually as part of a wider commitment to 'working with the community' – while others were content to rely on established mechanisms such as existing contacts with local organisations.

All commissioners interviewed identified groups who, they considered, were not currently being reached sufficiently, and these matched our hard-to-reach groups of single homeless people, young people, BME groups, asylum seekers, those who misuse substances, and travellers. They also mentioned offenders and those at risk of offending, although some commissioners felt that these should not or could not be consulted as they were undergoing forms of punishment for crimes committed.

Service users interviewed, for their part, didn't feel *they* could access commissioning groups generally because:

- neither group knew how to find, contact and engage with the other
- there were no channels of communication in existence
- there may be language barriers
- time and resources were lacking.

The commissioners also recognised that they and their personnel might not have the knowledge or be sufficiently skilled to reach and engage these groups. One respondent made it very clear that it was early days and that they would progress to these groups once the larger groups had been reached – for example, elderly people.

Current information is mostly qualitative, offering suggestions for service improvements, and some quantitative information such as waiting times and levels of use of facilities. Although this can contribute to service improvement it is not currently of use in terms of strategic planning or decision-making for services or Supporting People.

Good practice example

Southampton PCT, despite pressures to meet national standards, took the time to consult with clients to review and improve the services operating in a city-centre GP surgery.

The PCT conducted an in-depth consultation with the local community in a city-centre ward with a high BME population, when considering how to replace an existing general practitioner service that had closed on the retirement of its two doctors.

PCT staff undertook considerable outreach work to ensure that all sections of the community were given the opportunity to express their views on what kind and range of GP services were needed, how they should be delivered and where they should be located.

The PCT carried out ongoing consultation as it developed options, made decisions and began implementation – by using a mix of questionnaires, meetings, one-to-one interviews and written information provided in both English and other languages. The PCT also developed a database of 400 individuals and this will provide a basis for ongoing involvement in assessing the effectiveness of the service.

Most of the commissioners whom ROCC consultants interviewed said that clients' views were 'very influential' in the decision-making process, although they could provide little concrete evidence. Commissioners all said that information they obtained would need to be accurate, representational and independent, in order to be valid for use in the planning cycle. For example, as services are being reviewed under Supporting People and including input from clients, the commissioners felt that this could be expanded over time to ask more about strategic views.

Building trust was also important to commissioners, who felt that developing positive relationships with providers and their clients was crucial – for example, Portsmouth City Council's Supporting People staff have undertaken placements lasting several weeks in provider organisations to allow clients time to get to know them through informal dialogue about their thoughts and needs.

Case Study 4.8 shows how one Supporting People team took up the challenge of consulting with all the different service users groups in order to inform their five-year strategy development.

Case Study 4.8 Bath and North East Somerset (B&NES) Supporting People five-year strategy development
Consultation on draft proposals September 2004

In June 2004 the B&NES team launched the consultation programme for the development of the B&NES five-year strategy with an event for service providers.

At this event providers received a document containing all the needs-mapping information that had been gathered between December 2003 and May 2004, as well as a summary document and a set of outline draft proposals for each service user group.

The B&NES team invited providers to supply feedback and comments at the event and also set a deadline of 30 September 2004 for submission of written feedback on the outline draft proposals. Following the launch event, the B&NES team delivered a series of specifically tailored consultation events for service users. These events took place during July and August 2004 and are summarised below.

B&NES consulted all service user groups about the outline draft proposals for all service user groups, to ensure an optimum range of feedback. The B&NES team also sought the views of service users from across Bath and North East Somerset, rather than just from the Bath city area. All service users were assisted to complete a short questionnaire and were thanked for their time and input with a £5 gift voucher. Feedback was received from 126 service users in this way.

None of the commissioners had tried some of the more creative suggestions put forward by clients in the project, such as using websites or video, but they were open to the possibility of trying them. One example is the Wessex Youth Offending Team.

The Wessex Youth Offending Team has been piloting the use of View Point with their clients. View Point has been developed by an independent software company and is widely used to obtain information about individual clients of the Social Services Department and Youth Offending Team to measure users' satisfaction with services they receive. It uses a mix of interactive questions and games to encourage young people to provide information about themselves and the factors, including accommodation, that affect their behaviour.

How did commissioners' views tie in with service users' consultancy preferences?

It was clear from clients, providers and commissioners that clients taking part in specific strategic planning exercises should be paid or rewarded in a way that they could appreciate. For the Care Action Team it was in the form of a bursary; in other exercises it was vouchers.

Table 4.1 Bath summary of consultation methods and information gained

Service user group	Description of event(s)	Information provided	Facilitated by
Older people	Coffee mornings at sheltered housing schemes (7 events)	Summary of needs-mapping information and outline draft proposals translated into large print and audio tape	Supporting People team
Learning difficulties	Facilitated discussions carried out by specialist advocates/inter-preters (2 events)	Summary of needs-mapping information and outline draft proposals translated into words and pictures and audio tape	One-to-one
Mental health	Facilitated discussion (2 events)	Written summary of needs-mapping information and outline draft proposals	Rethink Supporting People team
Physical/sensory impairment	Facilitated discussions carried out by specialist advocates/inter-preters (individual service user interviews)	Summary of needs-mapping information and outline draft proposals translated into British Sign Language and recorded onto videotape	Centre for Deaf Studies Royal National Institute for the Deaf
Homeless families	Facilitated discussion (1 event)	Written summary of needs-mapping information and outline draft proposals	Supporting People team

Service user group	Description of event(s)	Information provided	Facilitated by
Rough sleepers	Facilitated discussion followed by lunch. The event was shared with rough sleepers, single homeless, drugs and alcohol and offenders (1 event)	Written and oral summary of needs-mapping information and outline draft proposals	Supporting People team/Supporting People providers
Vulnerable young people and care leavers	Facilitated discussion (2 events)	Written and oral summary of needs-mapping information and outline draft proposals	Supporting People team
Single homeless	See above for details of facilitated discussion. Also facilitated discussions in a number of hostels (4 events)	Written and oral summary of needs-mapping information and outline draft proposals	Supporting People team
Drugs and alcohol misusers	See above for details of facilitated discussion (1 event)	Written and oral summary of needs-mapping information and outline draft proposals	Supporting People team
Offenders	See above for details of facilitated discussion (1 event)	Written and oral summary of needs-mapping information and outline draft proposals	Supporting People team
Domestic violence	Facilitated discussions (2 events)	Written and oral summary of needs-mapping information and outline draft proposals	Supporting People team

SUMMARY

There are demonstrable barriers to service user consultation as presented by service users and service providers, and the authors would deem it the provider's duty to take the initiative in working to reduce these.

Where staff morale is low, service user consultation can be seen as yet another hoop to jump through – or, if well-presented by managers, as a very real piece of 'people' work to improve the services provided, and involve the users more fully.

Accordingly, where the right provider attitudes are present, service users would like to be involved in a variety of traditional and more creative methods of consultation, regardless of level, from day-to-day through to strategic planning.

Traditional methods of consultation:

- board or parallel boards
- questionnaires
- meetings – one-to-one and group
- conferences.

Additionally, more creative or modern methods such as

- newsletters
- websites
- creative writing

were raised as methods that either had worked successfully or could be tried, as service users had an interest in them.

Service users may prefer different methods for different times in their contact with you, e.g. if they are in crisis accommodation or at a crisis point in their lives, as compared with being on a more stable footing, perhaps receiving floating support in their own accommodation.

Table 4.2 summarises preferences for all the groups we have had experience of, and whether or not they consider these methods appropriate when they are a) in crisis or b) more stable.

Table 4.2 Summary of preferred methods of consultation for different groups

	Homeless		Drugs and alcohol		Women fleeing domestic violence		Young people		Roma and travellers		BME groups	
	Crisis	Stable	Crisis	Stable	Crisis	Stable	Crisis	Stable	Crisis	Stable	Crisis	Stable
Link to current networks					X			X	X	X		X
Community outreach												X
Staff advocacy	X		X		X		X			X		
Advocate for others		X		X		X		X				X
Day centre visits by commissioners	X	X										
Hostel visits by commissioners			X		X		X					
Forums		X		X				X				X
Drama			X				X					
Creative writing	X		X		X							
Newsletters	X						X					
Video	X						X					
IT	X	X		X	X	X	X	X				X

Workbook

This section helps you focus on which current activities can be used for consultation purposes, and offers the opportunity to think of new ideas.

- Are there any activities that service users currently undertake that could be adapted for consultation purposes or used to gain information for consultation purposes?
- Ask service users by what methods they would like to be consulted at the different levels.
- Ask service users what activities they would like to be involved with.
- Which methods and activities are you going to use and how often?
- How will you give them feedback?
- How will you gauge 'success'?
- What do service users think their training needs are and how will you meet these?

Table 4.3 Training needs analysis

	Current activities	New ideas	Resource implications	Training needs
Information				
Day-to-day				
Service development and policy				
Management				

CHAPTER 5

A Two-tier Model for Consultation for Strategic Planning

INTRODUCTION

The main focus of this chapter is on the two-tier model the authors have defined for primary and secondary consultation methods.

You can adapt both methods to apply to a range of client groups, service levels and needs. The authors have found both methods particularly useful for enabling more stable service users to consult with users in a crisis stage, helping them to feed their views into the strategic planning process, either in-house or linking with the local Supporting People team and core group.

The chapter also includes a detailed review of how the Hampshire and Portsmouth Supporting People teams applied the model and a report on a University of Portsmouth project to involve service users in educating students on the new social work degree.

Finally, as part of the workbook for this chapter, a generic outline policy and procedures for service user involvement are offered.

VALIDITY

Whether your organisation is large or small, the interest in strategic planning for Supporting People may initially be small, and the numbers willing to participate in this process even smaller, but their views need to be sought and are valid nonetheless. It is therefore important to seek solutions that are cost-effective and practical, yet as inclusive as reasonably possible, to allow those who want to be involved to take part in strategic decision-making processes in a variety of ways in line with their current life pressures.

The good practice group's developmental model of user involvement (see Box 3.2, p.61) demonstrates an increase in motivation in line with a decrease of personal crisis factors, and has a similarity with Maslow's hierarchy of needs.

(The model also has parallels with the former Office of the Deputy Prime Minister (ODPM)'s four levels of client consultation, where most (though not all) people are actively involved at the information and day-to-day levels, but fewest at the level of management or strategic planning.)

This demonstrates that clients are at their least able and interested to take part in strategic planning when 'in crisis', but as related needs are met they can take a wider perspective.

Where examples of effective consultation at levels 3 and 4 (see Box 3.2, p.62) were found, this tended to represent a progression from firm foundations of client involvement at levels 1 and 2. This is not to say, however, that client engagement increases in a purely linear fashion. Some individuals we interviewed had no interest in the day-to-day consultation, but wanted to talk strategy and service improvements with the 'movers and shakers' who they thought could take positive action.

It may not even be useful to define four discrete levels of consultation, since if we take the premise that the service user is at the centre of any work done with them then it can be just as valid to ask questions about the service offered as part of the build-up of a working relationship over time, and not necessarily as a separate or costly activity.

For example, a service user might sit on a board to make 'strategic' decisions, or be one of many service users with whom providers are able to develop positive working relationships such that questions around preferred service delivery methods can be asked as part of conversation. In this way it might be possible to ask all homeless visitors to a day centre over a year about, say, hostel provision in the area, and so a picture could be built up about needs and provision.

PRIMARY AND SECONDARY METHODS OF CONSULTATION

You may wonder whether clients should be expected to fit into the professionals' traditional style of consultation on strategic decision-making, i.e. attending committee and board meetings, and that there might be other more creative possibilities. When involving clients in committees or board meetings, there will always be concerns about literacy, understanding jargon, passive exclusion or tokenism; and, although you can successfully address these with a commitment to time and resources, there may be room for other approaches as well.

The authors have determined that there could be two types of consultation methods:

- *primary* – where the primary purpose is to consult

- *secondary* – group or shared activities that clients can participate in as part of their personal development (e.g. IT, art or drama projects), with the secondary purpose of providing channels for contributing to strategic decision-making.

This view was stimulated by a students' drama video project whose primary focus was to engage care leavers in a positive diversionary activity that could teach them camera skills. The resulting film also presented their views about the hostel and environment they lived in. This had a positive impact on the Supporting People children and families coordinator for Hampshire and has contributed to her current strategy.

Figure 5.1 shows a formal primary method for use with more stable service users. It can be used either in-house for an organisation with a variety of service user projects or groups, or externally where members are drawn from different geographical areas of a local authority and from different client groups. Members of this forum are supported and trained to consult with their peers or users of other local services in order to get their views in a more informal but still accountable way.

Here secondary methods can be used by individual user group representatives from any number of actual or virtual groups of hard-to-reach clients, to inform the primary means of consultation, the forum: representatives can be offered training and mentoring to act as conduits of information between commissioners and service users, utilising information gained from secondary consultation methods to inform the strategic planning forum. They can also

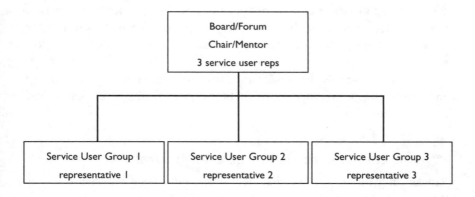

Figure 5.1 A two-tier model for primary and secondary consultation

develop relationships with commissioners and enable them to visit services to see clients where they feel best able to be consulted.

Costs

Although there are costs associated with involving service users at the strategic planning level, it is still a worthwhile investment. There are differences in funding streams and these will have an impact on the resources available to consult with clients of particular groups.

Traditional (primary) methods of consultation can be quite costly, as payment needs to be made for transport, attendance, parking, and refreshments for a number of people.

By using secondary methodologies, you could significantly reduce these costs, as these methods mean that fewer people need to be retained, trained and paid.

The authors recommended that providers and commissioners liaise to ensure knowledge of existing structures and mechanisms for consultation, especially with Black and minority ethnic (BME) groups, in order to prevent replication and consultation fatigue. Such structures and mechanisms include, for example, social cohesion units, gypsy Liaison Officers and Supporting People.

Development issues

As we saw in Chapter 4, the continued training of professionals (including service providers and commissioners) in valuing diversity, genuine equality of opportunity and anti-discriminatory practice would help to raise awareness of the issues facing individuals from BME groups needing inclusion into the wider community through improved access to housing-related support services.

Both professionals and service users need to be offered ongoing training and development in order to work better as individuals, as teams, and alongside each other.

What is common to all service user groups?

Reawakening professionals so that they become more open with clients lessens the 'them and us' divide.

Service users consistently indicated that they were more inclined to participate if they 'got on' with the staff, felt staff were 'human' and could trust them, while professionals in the ROCC good practice group felt refreshed by the level of openness that clients encouraged them to demonstrate in meetings, and felt that it speeded up the process of getting to know each other as people, rather than in the stark roles of 'staff' and 'client'.

So, in your work developing service user consultation and involvement, it is worth examining the nature of the 'professional boundaries' to see how far you need to observe personal safety and to what degree you can build up empathy so that you and your personnel can be professional and also human and trustworthy.

TOP TIPS FOR CLIENTS, COMMISSIONERS AND PROVIDERS

Clients do want:

- to be involved in ways that suit them
- respect, and to be treated as equals
- training, mentor/facilitation for strategic planning and decision-making concepts, systems, committee papers, etc., as well as training in assertiveness, group working, representation and advocacy
- feedback when they have been asked for views
- commissioners to come to them and see individual differences between groups and between people
- to be rewarded or paid for their input and often to receive travel expenses in advance.

Clients do not want:

- tokenism or to be patronised.

Clients may sometimes prefer:

- to speak for themselves
- anonymity
- to speak in their own group, rather than within a generic client consultation group (women in refuges).

Commissioners need to:

- offer a choice of consultation methods in order to engage clients i.e. flexible times/methods of involvement and consultation,

including development of current district inclusive forums and
working groups

- accept the validity of creative writing, drama, video and other
  projects as complementary qualitative information, but be
  prepared to collate into consistent and usable data
- go out [and say they want to] and see clients in their services
- offer practical partnerships for like agencies to set up independent
  user groups
- pay for consultation structures to be set up and run
- be clear about expectations, role and weight of views
- accept that some clients are happy for staff to speak for them
- offer payment or reward for contributions
- set up a mechanism for sharing good practice and establish
  common quality standards of user involvement in strategic
  planning.

Commissioners prefer:

- independently collated views, statistically valid surveys, etc.,
  which can set standards for providers to meet if they are
  consulting on their behalf.

Service providers:

- know they could/should do more – and would like assistance!

Service providers need to:

- develop a culture of commitment to client involvement and
  examine how real the barriers actually are
- demonstrate [as some do] an open leadership style, and
  commitment from the top of the hierarchy. If there is effective
  consultation at the basic levels of service delivery, such as in
  providing information, and in determining day-to-day activities, it
  is more likely that service users will be effectively consulted with
  and involved higher up – for example, in relation to management
  issues such as new service developments or recruitment and
  training of staff. Board member support as well as that of the chief

executive is essential for growing involvement at these higher levels

- assist clients' development to participate now or in the future in strategic planning exercises
- commit to working with clients to gain knowledge about how the clients want to be consulted, and not impose rigid structures on them
- develop structures alongside clients that clients want and can use
- provide clear expectations about what is offered and expected by clients
- plan the time, cost, and quality of client involvement with service providers
- engage in dialogue with commissioners to liaise with day centres/ open venues, etc., for open days, and invite commissioners in
- share good practice with each other.

It is recommended that providers and commissioners liaise to know what mechanisms already in place can be used for consultation purposes, in order to prevent replication and consultation fatigue. (Mechanisms may include, for example, social cohesion units, Gypsy Liaison Officers and Supporting People).

Commissioners and clients both believe that commissioners should go out to see clients where clients feel comfortable, and qualitative or creatively sourced information can complement quantitative data that could be collated by services on behalf of commissioners.

Designing a framework to ensure common standards for service user consultation processes enables service providers to establish and measure consistency and authenticity across different geographical areas and client groups.

By applying the core value of empowering vulnerable individuals to function as fully as possible within their community and involving them in effective consultation methods, service providers can apply users' views to help develop a fully integrated approach to strategic planning and decision-making for Supporting People.

It is also worth acknowledging here that there are real differences in funding streams, and these will have a greater or lesser impact on the resources available to consult with clients of particular groups. For example, PULSE, a group of service users that use drug services, has a presence at Drug and Alchohol Action Team meetings that users of alcohol services do not.

How independent are the views of hard-to-reach service users in strategic planning?

With Supporting People service reviews taking place, some clients are being consulted by Supporting People officers to ascertain their views about the services provided for them, and government guidelines recommend that 10 per cent of clients in a service are asked for their views.

As there is a potential risk of bias from service providers, commissioners are keen to see independently sourced consultation in order to gain what are considered the true views of clients, so methods will be needed to support this process.

Using a related service can cut across support services for particular groups – e.g. using day centres to ask clients' views of local provision – but generic service user groups were not a popular option for clients in this study. Ex-service users and more settled service users were the keenest to speak for others and be consulted about service developments and strategic planning, and they could be retained as expert witnesses or advocates, providing that pay or reward structures are put in place.

Clearly IT strategies could be of great benefit in reducing the cost of face-to-face interviews (for example, by using online questionnaires) and sharing good practice easily.

APPLYING THE MODEL IN HAMPSHIRE

Hampshire Supporting People team decided to fund the two-tier model proposed above by asking a group of service users to represent different clients' groups and geographical areas of Hampshire. The service users would attend meetings where a Hampshire Supporting People team member would provide information, and a facilitator would train them to consult in turn with other service users. The outcomes would directly inform the County Core Group, the highest level for decision-making for Supporting People in Hampshire.

How the Service User Reference Group (SURG) was set up

The team found it useful to contact known providers of Supporting People services to ask them to advertise the project using the eye-catching posters designed in-house. Team members then explained to interested parties the purpose and responsibilities involved in being a representative group member.

At the first meeting, five people from different parts of Hampshire, all with different backgrounds, attended. It had been agreed that membership should be as wide as possible, not just the hard-to-reach groups, as all groups needed representing in this first serious attempt to operate a mechanism for consultation at the strategic level. One person did not return after the first meeting and despite efforts to contact them we were unable to discover why.

Group membership

Although Hampshire is a large county, members come from the centre, north, west and east of the county, as Southampton and Portsmouth are separate unitary authorities.

The membership for the meetings held over the first year included:

- a young mother and survivor of domestic violence
- a young man with a physical disability living with support in the community
- a man with a history of alcohol problems and homelessness
- a man with learning difficulties living in a shared house.

A Hampshire Supporting People team member also attended in the mornings to present and explain the topic to be discussed. A minute-taker was present and the author's role was to facilitate the group discussions and provide training to the group.

Structure

Two sessions were planned between each County Core Group (CCG) meeting to:

- explain the topic
- enable members to consult other users
- finalise the views of the members before presenting these to the CCG.

It was decided to run meetings from 11.00am until 1.00pm to discuss the topic, have a lunch break, and then spend from 2.00pm to 4.00pm running training sessions for the group. The 11.00am start was useful, as it gave everyone sufficient time to ensure that they arrived promptly. Hot and cold drinks and biscuits were available all through the day, lunch was provided, and the group were told that they could have breaks as often as needed. This was important for service users' comfort and confidence, as most were not used to 'working' for long periods.

Topics

To date the group has been asked to:

- devise a consent form for Supporting People officers who need to access personal files as part of the validation visits to services
- discuss how to involve service users in the Supporting People review process
- review the introduction to the Hampshire Supporting People strategy document.

Consent form

It was explained why it was necessary for service users to give their consent for access to their files and the group then designed a simple draft form according to 'plain English' principles. The group discussed the relevant points within the meeting and then the users agreed to ask other service users for their views on the form.

At the following meeting, the service users explained that this had proved difficult, as many people they had spoken to did not understand what Supporting People was about, and, when it was explained, they were less than interested in taking the time to look over the proposed consent form. The group decided to keep the draft as it was and offer it to the CCG as something that could be rolled out to all services prior to their reviews taking place.

Involving service users in the review process

The team explained the Supporting People review process to the group, using simple diagrams.

The group then drafted a covering letter for all service providers to pass on to their service users, as it was felt that they would be the best conduits.

The group suggested that the Supporting People team could look at the possibility of funding a phone line and a user-friendly website as methods of receiving feedback about services from service users. This would be in addition to a simple questionnaire they also devised, which they felt asked questions most likely to elicit useful answers.

The draft questionnaire would ask:

1. How satisfied are you with the service you receive?

2. How involved were you in writing your support plan?

3. How safe do you feel?

4. If you have a problem how quickly can you get support?

5. Do you feel that your views are taken into account within your service?

6. How could your service be improved?

7. Is there anything else you would like to say?

The covering letter was as follows.

Box 5.1 SURG questionnaire covering letter

Dear [service user],

We are going to review your service [title of service] in the next three months and we would like your views on the service you receive.

You can give your opinion by:

• phoning [number]

• visiting the website at [website address]

• completing the enclosed questionnaire and returning it in the prepaid addressed envelope

• writing to us at [address details].

If none of these methods suit you, please call the phone number above and discuss better ways to meet your needs.

The Hampshire draft policy framework update

The team presented the draft policy framework to the group and explained that it had been drafted and redrafted by every group that the team had consulted, including eight district core groups, eight district inclusive forums and several subgroups.

The team explained that the policy framework had to be approved by the County Inclusive Forum and SURG. The group managed to simplify this document into plain English, and shorten it. Due to an oversight we did not encourage the members to take this out for consultation, although it is likely that they would have received little feedback, given the responses to the consent form.

Photography project

The team gave SURG members disposable cameras and asked them to record both positive and negative images of housing-related support services as part of a presentation to the CCG in the future.

Training

The major topic of interest to the group was improving their presentation skills, as they were all keen to develop themselves in this area before addressing the CCG. This would also have wider benefits in terms of generally improving the members' confidence, helping others to better understand them, and helping the members prepare for interviews in the future.

The group devised a good practice checklist for presentation skills to take away some of the anxiety about presenting. The authors listed what the presentation would contain, and ideas for how to present, as well as how to be prepared for all the things that could go wrong, along with what to do if they did!

This checklist is set out in Box 5.2 in the hope that it might provide inspiration for your consultation methods!

Box 5.2 SURG presentation skills session

It was agreed that the session should start with a comprehensive description of SURG and what had been achieved so far, covering the following items:

I. What we want to tell the CCG

- what SURG is (the attendants, the services they use and where they live)

- what SURG has done so far (three meetings, ROCC newsletter, consent form, letter and questionnaire for review process)

- the consent form

- the letter and questionnaire for involving service users in the review process.

---

2. Presentation methods

The following resources and methods were available for effective presentation:

- overhead projector slides/Microsoft PowerPoint software
- flipcharts and pens
- talking
- written reports/leaflets
- photos
- formal – taking questions at the end
- informal – to ensure more of a discussion as the presentation proceeds.

3. Presentation skills

The following considerations were identified as being helpful in ensuring the most effective presentation:

- dress – comfortable/smart/casual
- voice – clear, loud enough, varied tone, not too fast or slow
- attitude – positive, happy
- eye contact – make sure you look at everyone
- posture – stand up straight, do not fidget
- language – do not use jargon unless you explain it
- subject – know the subject and be convincing
- message – should be clear, simple and easy to understand.

4. Avoiding problems

If you want to make a confident start to a presentation:

- prepare your information well beforehand
- use prompt cards if you think you might forget something
- do not eat anything or drink gassy drinks too close to your presentation
- stay calm and relaxed – take things slowly – take deep breaths if necessary
- concentrate on what you are saying at all times and remain focused.

If you do not know something, be honest about it, and offer to find out and report back later.

Project successes

The authors felt that the SURG project had produced a number of successful outcomes:

- a consistent attendance and participation from group members
- a high level of learning about complex issues
- learning to take part in discussions
- learning presentation skills and demonstrating them
- increasing confidence
- increasing trust and social skills
- contribution of very good ideas
- maintaining awareness of keeping language simple
- remembering to slow down and ensuring everyone understands.

Despite the different backgrounds and skills levels of the SURG membership, it has proved to be a very supportive group. In fact, one member returned to the group after suffering a relapse in his health, despite missing two meetings.

It took the team a long time to explain the principles of the Supporting People programme, the reasons for and processes of reviewing services and the structure of the various district and county groups. The group has demonstrated ability to see things at a variety of levels, including the strategic level, and members have certainly developed their thinking, planning and communication skills.

One member (Douglas) attended a County Core Group meeting, delivered a PowerPoint presentation and answered questions to a large group of powerful strangers. He was congratulated on the standard of the presentation and his use of humour. This was the text of his presentation:

Box 5.3 Douglas's presentation

I am Douglas Mallett (28); I have got a physical disability down my right side. I have been living in a supported housing flat (Hyde Housing Association) for two years in Fleet, which I look after by myself with the aid of support workers coming every day.

I learned from my Supported Housing Officer that ROCC was inviting a group of service users to help other service users to get more out of their service providers by working with Supporting People who fund the services, so I jumped at the chance of becoming a member of the SURG Group.

I like meeting different people from different backgrounds and interacting with them, discussing about how to improve the way Supporting People do things. Supporting People asked us to design a questionnaire so they can get feedback from other service users about their service provider, that I enjoyed doing. I feel that the SURG Group is an excellent idea and benefits many types of service users. I have learned some inside knowledge about the way that the service providers work and are funded. I am proud to be a member of SURG and the work it does.

Communication

This is what another member, Kelly, wrote for a newsletter:

Box 5.4 Kelly's newsletter article

SURG, standing for Service Users' Reference Group, had their first meeting on 19th April 2004, and if you haven't heard of us yet then you will!!!

We are five individuals receiving support from service providers under the Supporting People programme in Hampshire, who were chosen by ROCC to represent the voices of the service users. In the following newsletters you will get to meet the rest of SURG but I will begin with explaining a bit about myself and what we have done so far.

I am a single mother who has had a lot of help and support from Southern Focus Trust as a result of domestic violence. We were lucky enough to be housed in bed and breakfast accommodation and stayed there for 10 months sleeping and living in a single room. This meant that the support I received was vital to me from help with solicitors, benefit forms to having a key worker who was easily reached and would be there for me. There were problems along the way which made me realize that as my own situation got better I would like to be involved in ensuring others get the same benefit.

The group has so far looked at the current problems of consent forms for service reviewers to see our files, for example wording, what is necessary? Together we gave our views and produced a new form that hopefully will be distributed between the providers. Each of the group members then took the consent form back to other service users to get feedback and wider opinions covering groups in most of Hampshire.

> Also discussed were the review process of individuals and their differ-ent client groups, client files, confidentiality and service user involvement, as well as trying to find solutions and methods of contacting and involving the service user.
>
> We hope to be able to attend future County Inclusive Forums to share our ideas with you all.

Work in progress

The group's development will be reviewed in the near future. Kelly also made a presentation to the County Inclusive Forum as a method of better publicising the group and seeking stronger networks for accessing service users available for consultation.

Conference speaking

As the group has become better known, other providers have contacted them (e.g. Advance Housing and Support) some members were asked by the Centre of Cost Effectiveness to talk about SURG at a conference for service providers in January 2005, which went extremely well. Presentations by service users Kelly and Drac were very well received by the large audience.

Future developments

For the Hampshire model we are shortly to review what has gone well and what would be improved if we were to be refunded for a further year.

The one thing that has not been done consistently as the group has developed is to consult with other service users about the issues that have taken time to work on in the group session – for example, the Hampshire strategic plan. SURG was not clear whether this topic would have benefited from even more consultation than it had already received, and, in terms of editing a document into plain English, it did not necessarily require further consultation.

It was, however, very useful for the Supporting People representative to receive the group's views as perhaps typical rather than representative. Where this group will be able to come into its own is on the topic of how to engage service users more fully in the service review process.

Recently group member Kelly delivered a presentation to the service providers attending the County Inclusive Forum. In the presentation she high-lighted SURG's existence and offered to make links into their service users' groups formally or informally, depending on the developmental stage the service is at. She suggested that they could link by either geography or client group, depending on how services express their interest and with facilitation by SURG representatives visiting and talking with their service users.

PORTSMOUTH MODEL

The Portsmouth Supporting People team also contracted to run a SURG along the same lines, but initially for a shorter period than Hampshire.

The group is still running currently due to its success in 2005. At the first meeting the Supporting People co ordinator explained the Supporting People agenda to a keen team of five, with particular reference to taking part in service reviews and validation visits. Once staff vacancies were filled, the Portsmouth Supporting People staff were keen for service users to assist them with service reviews, in particular the validation visits. In addition SURG members have got to know each other, the Supporting People staff, facilitator and minute-taker. Within the team, the staff, facilitator and minute-taker and the SURG service users have all developed rapport and work very well together.

At the second meeting, the Supporting People representative explained the local strategy and asked the group to focus on where they felt there were gaps in service provision. The group spent time outlining what they felt worked well, what could be improved, and where there were gaps in provision in relation to housing and support services for people who were:

- homeless
- at risk of re-offending
- families
- teenagers.

SURG was asked for its views on the standards of building and service quality, and how best to communicate with service users in general. The group also looked at interviewing skills, decided who they were going to ask for their views about the priorities, and agreed questions they would use for the basis of informal discussion. The questions are listed below:

1. What Supporting People services have you used in the last five years? (Accommodation and Support Services). Give examples.

2. Were your needs met? (Accommodation and/or Support)

3. How long did it take to get the service/accommodation?

4. Were you satisfied with speed of 'move on'? If not, what were the reasons?

5. What could be improved?

6. What else can be done to help meet your needs?

7. What is the biggest barrier you came up against?

8. Is there a gap or any gaps in services?

9. Are there any new services needed?

10. Where did you find out about services?

11. Are you happy with your accommodation?

12. Are you happy with your support services?

SURG service user members contacted 60 other service users, who gave their views either through the semi-structured interviews or through completing the questionnaire, once it had been explained to them by the SURG service user members.

Views that the SURG service users have collected from the Foyer (for young and homeless people), from Kingsway House (for drug and alcohol problems) and from Southern Focus Trust (a charity for most service user groups), as well as from street homeless people, are summarised in Table 5.1.

The biggest areas for complaint were the slowness of 'move on', and a belief that agencies could probably work better together.

The group also reported that quality of staff was an issue. Young people and those with substance misuse issues felt that they built rapport more easily with people closer to their own age who had experienced similar difficulties. It was felt by service users that there was a range of staff in the profession, from 'brilliant' to of 'little help and support'.

SURG members suggested that service users could be more involved in staff training. One of the biggest barriers faced by those seeking employment was having a criminal record, even if they had firsthand and past experience of being homeless or using substances, alcohol or drugs.

James Lovelock, service user on the SURG group, wrote the following for this book and for a ROCC newsletter:

> I have attended three out of the four meetings so far and we have covered the local strategy. We threw around ideas to find out where or if there are any gaps in any of the services. Following the ideas that we came up with, we produced questions to take to service users to find out their input. I found it was easier to make it into a questionnaire so I could get 10 people to fill it out at the same time rather than interviewing separately. If they needed to ask any questions I was there to help them through it.

I found that the service users were very keen to interact with me as an ex-service user because I feel that they relate a lot better with me because they don't see me as so much of an authority figure. They respect the fact that I have been where they are.

The information that I got back from it was very useful in the following meeting. For the next group meeting we have been asked to go back to service users and ask questions about communication between services and this time I will go to a different service to find out unbiased information again.

I have really enjoyed being involved with the SURG meetings. I found it interesting and also it's nice to see some of the information not only being put to use but also that it can make a difference to people using the service now and in the future. I would like to work in this field and I would like to make a difference if I could. I have a lot of knowledge about services I have used myself and already see some gaps. I hope it carries on into next year so that more service users have a voice and benefit from what we are doing.

Communication strategy

The group has been asked to help develop this, and get other service users' views. Essentially what is required is the following:

- What sort of information do potential or actual service users need?
- How should this be presented?
- Where should this be made available?

For example, James Lovelock said that he had always felt there was a need for a directory of services. It was agreed that a directory that listed direct access services, supported housing schemes, and linked or related support services, would be very useful if could be produced. The group agreed that it would be happy to do this if Supporting People agreed to it. The directory would be cross-referenced and would also list statutory agencies. It was also suggested that large maps and pocket versions should be made available in a format similar to information for tourists. This would then be available at all the places where people go to find information – for example, at the library. The map would show where the services were, and transport routes, as people often had no idea how far apart services were or how to get there.

Box 5.5 shows the questionnaire that will be used as a basis for future interviews.

Future funding has been agreed so that the group will be able to continue this work. Other achievements of SURG include involving service users in the

Table 5.1 Summary of priorities

Description of needs for each group

	Homeless people	At risk of re-offending	Families	Teenagers
Housing and support	Cut waiting list and move on (timescales) Image Safety Support activities Keyworker as soon as needed and being informed of each case Reviews of needs/support More direct access beds Portsmouth City Council to set targets for length of stay Source of information of appropriate services	Prescribing heroin to addicts could reduce treatment numbers Budgeting Diversion and training activities Resettlement from prison Buddying system/befriending Self build schemes and council paying wage for them to do it Work experience Advice and direction e.g. Sothern Focus Trust and advocacy	Appropriate accommodation Link with education Floating support Tenancy support Budgeting Help for parents and children individually and together	Prevention Safe accommodation Childcare and training Respite Increase attractiveness of accommodation available for young women and babies as prevention
Quality of services	Service users assist staff training to improve service quality Reliable staff Quick to fix problems Trust them Genuinely try to help Help to move on/in quickly Constancy of keyworkers is important for service users to build up trust			

Building standards	Choice of food important
	Some places do not offer safety and privacy
	Cramped bedrooms in foyer
	Mill house mixed male and female
	Drug and alcohol users around the buildings causing trouble
	A nightshelter was very bad, much improved now
Communi cation issues	Between services needs improving – in order to orientate the person in to the right services
	Booklet for all those who may need it listing agencies, map etc.
	Homelessness links with other services: health, education, for prevention of homelessness, teen pregnancies etc.
	Sex sense very good, expand it

review process, amending and improving a variety of policies, and making contributions to newsletters and annual reports. Documents that have been 'SURG approved' are given the logo – a yellow tick – and registered with ROCC.

Box 5.5 Questions for service users to inform communication strategy for Portsmouth Supporting People

1. What information do you need in order to access the Supporting People services you require (e.g. opening hours, service type)?

2. How could this best be presented to you (e.g. plain English, colour-coded sections, etc.)?

3. Would a directory of services be useful?

4. If yes, what should be included in it?

5. Would a map be useful?

6. Where should all this information be made available (e.g. library, job centre, etc.)?

UNIVERSITY OF PORTSMOUTH MODEL

One of the authors was asked to work with the university's social work department to develop a sustainable model for service user and carer participation at all levels for the new social work degree, as it was felt that the experiences of service users and carers would provide excellent depth to the course material already offered by the academic staff.

The participation of users and carers in social services committees is already seen as valid and important, as indicated by Jones (1995), where good practice guidelines were drawn up following a survey of practice on user and carer participation in social services committees.

The guidelines point out that users and carers contribute views and perspectives based on their own experience. They should not necessarily be regarded as representing others, or made to feel responsible for representing their peer group.

> People may be representative, or typical users, but not the representatives of other users. The legitimacy of their views rests in their personal experience, and it is likely that those in similar circumstances will share much of that experience. The roles in which people participate, and their responsibilities, need to be discussed and made clear for all concerned. (Barnes *et al.* 1997)

The involvement of service users and carers in the social work degree

There are five main areas where lecturers felt service users and carers could be involved in the social work degree and post-graduate course(s):

1. student recruitment and selection – from short-listing and formulation of interview questions, to interviewing potential social work students

2. teaching – service users and carers could deliver teaching input to small or large groups in the classroom using a variety of methods:

   - addressing a class
   - working in a small group
   - working indirectly, via video
   - contribution to teaching material
   - using drama to demonstrate their experiences
   - inviting students into their service to explain what it does

3. fitness for practice panels – the panel gives staff, users and carers the opportunity to assess students' fitness to go out on a managed placement in an area of social care. The students have an interview and the panel asks them about the action they would take when faced with a case study. Practice panels are held in May and September

4. writing case studies – for use in practice panels and teaching, so new ones are needed over the year

5. course management – carers and users could observe and feed back information at the highest level of management of the new social work degree.

Training

University staff offered and provided training where requested, to enable people to take part to the best of their ability in these activities.

Payment

Monthly meetings

The university agreed that travel expenses would be reimbursed within reason for those in the Portsmouth area. Those living out of the area might need to negotiate this with the university. So far it has only been the care mileage of one of the carers who brings two others in the car. The university has a taxi account and organises pre-paid rides to and from meetings, providing they know a few days before the meeting to make the advance booking.

Activities

Payment was available at £5 per hour, or equivalent in vouchers, in four-hour blocks of activity.

METHOD

The authors decided to adapt the two-tier model to reflect that there would be a permanent but perhaps small group of service users and carers who would meet monthly with the two key staff, and others would attend when relevant or requested to do so. It was also planned to collect a database of interested parties who would like to be involved in certain activities only, and not necessarily attend regular meetings.

A first date, venue and time were set and a poster designed to go out to all agencies that staff and the authors collectively were aware of, including network organisations that it was hoped could pass on the information and display the colourful posters prominently.

Over 25 people attended the first meeting, partly thanks to the fact that the University of Portsmouth had formerly operated a service user group, although it had only operated for a short time. The university staff were keen to resurrect this group and to maintain it in the longer term. The intention this time was to sustain interest and be able to offer training and involvement over the whole area of the new degree, as well as to consolidate the excellent work achieved by Teri Rogers in drawing on carers and service users for the post-qualifying award for social workers in childcare.

During the five meetings that took place between May and November 2004 there were often newcomers, and therefore the university staff always took the time to explain the purpose as follows.

- The University of Portsmouth wants to involve users of social services in statutory and voluntary sector agencies, as well as carers, in the new social work degree.
- The university wants to set up a structure for consulting with and training service users and carers, in order to continuously improve the training and development of students on the new social work degree.

- The first deadline was interviewing students in November.

It was decided that one of the authors would take meeting minutes and send these out to all service users and carers on the database as it evolved, either by post or email, as preferred by group members. It was ensured that the minutes were brief summaries of discussions held and outcomes, and that they went to all on the database so that everyone was kept informed, regardless of whether or not they were able to attend meetings.

To date, there are 45 service users and carers on the database, and approximately 20 turn up at each meeting. They enjoy the social activity of meeting together, and because the meetings take place between 5pm and 7pm, we offer the group hot and cold drinks and a sandwich supper.

The views of the users and carers make a real difference, and several have already taken part in interviewing students and sitting on the fitness to practice panels. Some of the young people have shared their experiences in the classroom, which prompted queues afterwards to ask them further questions. Most important, perhaps, these young people felt very accepted by the students, who chatted with them and took them for coffee in the break times.

Progress

A code of conduct was developed by the group, and each meeting focused on one of the following five areas: student recruitment and selection, teaching, fitness for practice panels, writing case studies and course management. Different members of university staff attended, to explain their requirements.

Code of conduct

The group agreed the following code of conduct for all members.

- There should be no discrimination at all on age, sex, ethnicity, religion, or on any other grounds.
- There should be equal respect for all.
- The expertise of users and carers should be recognised.
- Ensure that everyone is heard.
- Ensure that all forms of communication are valuable.
- Treat people as you would like to be treated.
- Do not repeat others' judgements.
- Do not patronise people.

- Students are not to probe into personal issues and staff are to uphold this.
- Establish clear boundaries from the very beginning.
- Do not to single out students for criticism.
- Value individuals.

Shortlisting and selection of new students

At a meeting focussing on selection of social work students, one of the social work lecturers asked for views on the selection process and questions asked at interview.

She explained that she shortlists applications against set criteria, and allocates interviews. The week before interviews she sends out copies of the applications to those who will be interviewing, and has previously had a pool of people to draw from in case of short-notice absences. The interview panel has consisted of a service user or carer, a tutor, and a social worker in practice. There are usually three panels running at once and one set of three panels running per month from December to June. The interview is structured around a set of questions the panel ask. They then discuss each candidate at the end of their interview and make a decision about whether or not they are fit to practice social work on a placement.

Information about all applicants is kept confidential, and service users and carers have a room where they can chat, prepare and eat lunch, etc. The lecturer explained that they had not usually paid the users and carers in the past, owing to benefit issues, but had provided a letter of reference instead. The list of questions was circulated and discussed. Service users and carers contributed their suggestions and changes to questions and these were all taken up by the university team. Nine service users and carers offered to participate on the interview panels and were happy with the initial short-listing process.

Involvement in teaching

Another social work lecturer attended a meeting to ask service users and carers if they would be prepared to talk to new students in their first week of term, as this coincided with Mental Health Week. He stated that World Mental Health Day was on 10 October at the end of Mental Health Week, and that this was also the first week of term for new students.

Some group members were willing to take part, but the date was changed, meaning that not all those who wanted to were able to take part. He later said that it had been very useful for new students to hear the experiences of those who were able to come, and that students had been able to contribute to a discussion about risk assessment. This had provoked a discussion in the meeting about what might be holding back social workers practising now (such as risk assessment and red tape), and how this could be positively framed to help the learning of new social work students. It was agreed that a good social worker is one who is able to:

- give time
- be reliable
- remember you.

There had also been positive outcomes for some young people, e.g. getting their own flat. As mentioned previously, social services now demonstrates more respect to young people whenever they move by providing them with a suitcase or bag of their choice, rather than simply a black binbag: this shows consideration and empathy.

Young people present said that social work students might learn better if they went to visit young people in their territory, rather than have young people come into their classroom, and this opened up much more creative views on teaching and learning that are removed from the traditional classroom lecture. Service users felt that such visits might also increase students' confidence, since social workers were often afraid of service users, as they had not necessarily gained enough experience or core skills to develop positive working relationships and good rapport with their clients.

Fitness for practice panel

The panel allows staff, users and carers the opportunity to assess students' fitness to go out on a managed placement in an area of social care. These panels are held in May at the end of the first year and act as a quality control for students before they go out on placement. In order to be seen as fit to practice, students must:

- pass all 'year one' work
- shadow a social worker in practice for five days, and write an assignment on this between January and April.

A tutor also writes a report on each student's study and practice. The job of the panel is to read this report and interview the student about their knowledge to date.

The student also reads a case study and then applies his or her knowledge to it. The case study concentrates on ethics, anti-discriminatory practice, child development, and issues affecting adults and communication.

A service user who had attended a previous panel noted that the same case study was used for all students, so that by the end of the day students had shared the details with each other, making it theoretically easier for the students seen later in the day. Therefore it was decided that a variety of case studies or scenarios was needed.

Fifteen service users and carers have taken part in fitness for practice panels so far and have been able to provide useful questions to test students' learning. Another very useful activity to get involved with would be developing a range of scenarios to be used in future.

Conclusion

The university staff have seen this initiative as an enormous success in terms of using more creative teaching methods than those traditionally used in universities.

University staff, service users and carers all agreed that evening meetings were the best option, as the university staff were involved in their teaching jobs and some service users and carers have daytime responsibilities.

There appears to have been a good coming together of the staff, service users and carers, and sometimes students come along to take part also. It is likely that this group will continue to be successful as members' potential barriers have been reduced as far as possible.

SUMMARY

Clearly, we can use a variety of methods to involve service users at the higher levels of consultation, providing we reduce the barriers and put the enablers in place to allow maximum comfort and participation by group members.

For commissioners of services such as Supporting People, a two-tier model of consultation works, providing sufficient time and energy is committed to supporting and training service users and helping them to feel that their participation is sufficiently rewarding and respected.

For a university social work department, including service users and carers as a planning group and wider virtual group of willing participants to contribute to the selection, teaching and assessment of students has already made a significant difference to the experience of students who will, when qualified, enter the field as professionals.

Workbook

There is a continuous improvement loop in consultation.
You should now be able to:

- review your plan/strategy to date
- establish where you are now compared to when you started
- isolate the problems and determine how you overcame them
- define what still needs doing
- ensure that you have a system for reviewing the progress you are making
- establish ways in which you can advertise and share your good practice so that others can learn from you.

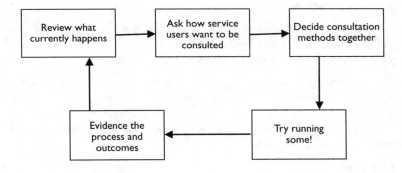

Figure 5.2 Continuous improvement feedback loop

Box 5.6 Service user involvement – policy and procedures

Introduction

This policy sets out to demonstrate the commitment of this organisation to providing genuine opportunities open to service users to be consulted with and as fully as possible involved in the running of their services, and that we have made all reasonable efforts to encourage service users to take advantage of these opportunities.

Underlying this policy is our ethos of person-centred development and commitment to maximising each service user's potential to live as independently as possible, and be as active a citizen as they wish to be in the community. This ethos also includes welcoming a diversity of backgrounds, views and opinions, coupled with a commitment to anti-discriminatory practice in all aspects of the service.

In order to recognise the value of enabling the individual to have a voice, the organisation will invest reasonable time, energy and money in developing this policy and its related procedures.

Aim

Our policy is to enable service users to be involved in the running of their services as far as possible in the following four areas:

1. information

2. day-to-day activities

3. planning, policy and performance measurement

4. service management.

We expect that involvement of users in the service will be an aspect of continuous development and that methods of consultation may change and vary in line with service users' wishes and requirements.

If this means a change in organisational culture or staff attitudes, we are committed to this change and will ensure availability of appropriate training and development for all staff and volunteers working in the service.

We will explain our policy and procedures to service users in the ways most appropriate for them.

Managers

It is the responsibility of managers to ensure that all new staff thoroughly understand this policy and have signed up to it prior to confirmation in their post.

It is the responsibility of managers to ensure that all established staff understand this policy and have signed up to it following a mutually agreed period of time.

Procedures
Strategy

We will develop this strategy via a variety of consultation methods to ascertain how users would like to be involved and then develop a practical strategy to enable and ensure service user involvement in all aspects of their service.

We will be guided by *Supporting People: A Guide to User Involvement for Organisations Providing Housing-related Support Services* (ODPM 2003) and

Reflecting the Needs and Concerns of Black and Minority Ethnic Communities in Supporting People ((DTLR) and the Regions 2002), where this is helpful.

Whilst we recognises the right of service users to not participate in consultation exercises, we will ensure that the opportunities are available for any service users who choose to be involved at any stage.

We will ensure that training, mentoring and advocacy are available as far as possible to enable service users to participate as fully as they wish.

Information

We will consult with service users about the information we put out about their services to ensure that we are advertising and explaining the services in a way that is understandable to potential and current users.

All our internal and external information targeted at service users will be in plain English, translated into other languages or symbols where appropriate, and be comprehensible to service users. We will place information where potential and actual service users can see it, and will promote dialogue between professionals and users via appropriate access channels such as telephone numbers, named staff, availability times, etc.

A measurable outcome is that service users' feedback is incorporated as information and is updated and advertised.

Day-to-day activities

We will consult with service users about the day-to-day activities that take place in the service to enable them to choose and decide what they want to do and how they want to be involved, where such activities are reasonable and risks have been assessed.

A measurable outcome shall be that users are satisfied with the choice and range of activities they are involved in on a day-to-day basis, and that they have been involved in planning such activities.

Planning, policy and performance measurement

We will consult with service users about the planning of their services, policy development and changes, and how we measure performance.

We will involve service users in staff recruitment and training activities as well as shaping policy and setting and reviewing quality standards. We will measure our own performance by how many users become involved, and sustain that involvement, in service planning, recruiting staff, devising policy and measuring performance. Service users will be consulted about quality standards we set and monitor in these areas.

Service management

We will consult with service users about how they want to be involved in service management and will put processes in place that enable users to be involved in the management of their service at board or equivalent level.

This will be evidenced by structures set up, used and improved for service users to have an involvement in aspects of managing the service.

Staff

All staff will demonstrate attitudes and behaviours that value and encourage service users' views and opinions at all levels of consultation and in all aspects of the service.

All staff will use a variety of methods to seek views, including traditional and more creative methods, depending on the wishes and abilities of service users to engage and communicate.

Methods

The organisation may select methods from the lists below, or others requested or suggested by staff and service users.

Primary methods

- one-to-one discussion
- small groups
- service-wide forum
- questionnaires
- representatives' groups
- representatives on board
- parallel board.

Secondary methods

- creative writing
- art
- drama
- video diary
- photography
- newsletters
- IT message boards/email.

Enabling participation

We will ensure that service users receive adequate preparation, training, mentoring and advocacy support, to enable them to participate as fully as possible.

We will seek to enable service user participation as far as possible by responding to service users' needs as far as reasonably possible, some examples being:

- using plain English, and translations where necessary
- minimising and explaining jargon
- seeking mutual agreement for meeting times and venues
- providing transport and childcare where needed.

All staff will obtain service users' consent to take part in consultation exercises and will explain fully the reasons why their views are being sought and are valued.

We will provide feedback and clear explanations for decisions made that have utilised service users' views in the process.

Confidentiality

Where possible and/or appropriate, we will collect and/or collate service users' views anonymously to protect individual user identity and will explain this to service users.

Payment

Where we identify that consultation with service users is extra to those processes that they will carry out in their daily lives as a matter of course in the services they receive, we will make a payment and/or reward. For example, we would pay or reward service users for attending a board meeting to represent the collective views of other service users.

We will discuss payment and reward methods with service users and agree these within the organisation before any such consultation takes place.

Changes

This organisation works within an ethos of continuous improvement, so we will monitor and review this policy and related procedures regularly, and amend these as appropriate and/or in line with new legislation.

This policy and set of procedures have been read, discussed, understood and signed up to today [date] by:

Employee:

Line Manager:

If you feel it is an appropriate time to do so, you can now write your policy and procedures for service user consultation. Above is a generic outline, which you can adapt with your staff and service users to fit your own service, having consulted with them about it first!

CHAPTER 6

The Young Men's Christian Association (YMCA)

INTRODUCTION

In this chapter we will look at the work of the global youth charity, the Young Men's Christian Association. The YMCA is a good example of an organisation that works with hard-to-reach groups such as young people who are homeless, in prison, have drug or alcohol problems, or are from black and minority ethnic (BME) groups.

After an overview of the YMCA across the world, we will look at the work of Terry Eckersley – one of the authors of this book – who was housing manager at Southampton YMCA, and is now chief executive of Woking YMCA. Terry's work with the YMCA offers an excellent example of how to include and involve service users at all levels in an organisation.

Throughout its 160-year history, the YMCA has attracted, worked with, and transformed the lives of what we now call 'new user groups' and 'client bases'. With its proven track record and huge worldwide network, the YMCA is able to take hold of new legislation and innovative ideas and make them work across the world. From its founding to the present day, the YMCA has been a champion of young people, and has involved them in the creation, development and running of its programmes.

WHAT IS THE YMCA?

The YMCA is a leading Christian charity committed to supporting all young people, particularly in times of need.

YMCA England supports and represents the work of nearly 150 YMCAs providing professional and relevant services that make a difference to the lives of young people in over 250 communities. The YMCA reaches out to more than one million young people each year, working with them at every stage of their lives and offering support when and where they need it most.

Vision

The YMCA's vision is of an inclusive Christian movement, transforming communities so that all young people truly belong, contribute and thrive.

Work

Founded 160 years ago, the YMCA in England builds on a long history of providing a place for young people to find acceptance, community and activity. It does this by offering high quality services in seven integrated areas:

- Housing and homelessness – the YMCA provides safe places for young people to live, grow and learn, particularly when they face difficult times in their lives.
- Health and physical activity – the YMCA offers projects and programmes that encourage people to be active and healthy.
- Crime prevention and youth justice – the YMCA leads cutting-edge work with young people in prisons and with people who have been offenders. It also works to lower the numbers of young people who are involved in crime or become victims of crime.
- Education, skills and extended schools – the YMCA provides a wide range courses that offer a less formal option than school, college or university and help young people gain skills and qualifications. It also works in schools and colleges to offer courses and clubs before, during and after classes.
- Training, work and financial management – the YMCA offers a range of services to help young people get better jobs, and stick with them. It also encourages young people to learn to look after their money better, and offers job-specific training courses such as national vocational qualifications (NVQs).
- Citizenship and advocacy – the YMCA helps young people to be more involved in making choices and to have their voices heard on issues that are important to them.
- Parenting and family – the YMCA offers services that help people to understand what good family relationships are and provides care for children and parenting classes in schools.

Every YMCA association in England is autonomously managed and works to meet the specific needs of young people in its local community.

THE WORLD ALLIANCE OF YMCAs

As the oldest voluntary organisation in the world, the World Alliance of YMCAs is an umbrella association that supports and has input from over 12,000 YMCA branches and has around 30 million members.

Its main focus is to develop and maintain the YMCA across the globe, particularly YMCAs in the southern hemisphere. Alongside its main aim, it also particularly promotes the participation and involvement of young people and women in the organisation.

The scope of the alliance's work is vast, and, with its the broad range of user groups, it is hard to imagine a network of organisations and partnerships that has a wider reach.

The alliance also provides an important and influential platform for international political and social debate. In recent years it has discussed many of the world's most prominent issues such as interfaith dialogue, the Israeli–Palestine conflict, world debt, the nuclear arms race, and the US embargo of Cuba.

Many YMCAs in England have partnerships with YMCA centres and projects across the world. These mutually beneficial connections usually offer exchange programmes that strengthen the YMCA's international role and profile.

INTERNATIONAL RELIEF AND DEVELOPMENT

Y Care International, the international relief and development agency of the YMCA in the UK and Ireland, also offers a worldwide framework for the YMCA, funding and supporting development projects that empower young people and their communities in Africa, Asia, Latin America and the Middle East.

In each country where Y Care operates, it works with local agencies with the aim of involving user groups to design their own programmes to meet their needs.

The service user groups that Y Care works with are varied and increasing. Its current programmes are focused on work with street children and children forced into labour at an early age. It also concentrates on work with girls and young women, people with disabilities, refugees and other displaced people.

Its areas of work are similarly broad, encompassing HIV and Aids awareness, citizenship, post-conflict and emergency relief, rehabilitation and justice for young people, youth leadership, representation, skills development and employment.

It offers a major programme that encourages young people from the UK and Ireland to become active global citizens and campaign on issues they care passionately about.

YMCA'S WORK IN DOMESTIC SITUATIONS

The YMCA also works to promote positive parenting and good family relationships. It helps young people and families during times of transition – when young people move out or back home – and offers childcare support to help parents balance work and home life. It also mediates between families in dispute or serious crisis.

Many young people have disruptive backgrounds and family lives owing to divorce, step-families, absent parents, and a lack of affection from their parents – whether natural, step-, adopted or foster parents. Children and young people can be deeply affected by these factors, which can lead to high emotional fallout – one in nine young people aged 16 runs away from their family home.

One of the guiding forces behind the YMCA's work offering supported housing to young people who would otherwise be homeless is to encourage them to participate in the running of the YMCA. Across the YMCA, service users take an active part in the day-to-day running of their accommodation. Many YMCAs have networks that encourage dialogue between staff and residents and hold regular forums to allow young people to speak out, such as residents' committees and tenants' forums. The YMCA aims to put the views, opinions and experiences of young people at the forefront when structuring its services to best serve their needs.

'EXCLUDE ME IN'

Aiming to meet the needs of young people who are socially disadvantaged and excluded, 'Exclude me in' offers programmes that uncover the root causes of exclusion. Its aim is to give service users the skills, self-belief and attitude to be able to play a positive role in the community. It works by identifying an individual's needs and priorities, which can then be used to direct them to play a more active, inclusive role in their community.

The YMCA helps young people to find supported housing and accommodation after a row or break-up with their family. The young people will often want to live near their family home, with the hope that they can restore family relations. A YMCA support worker will play a vital role in this process, and is often the first to contact the family and begin the process of reconciliation.

To fulfil their potential, young people need to be stimulated and challenged. Through its programmes, the YMCA offers young people a sense of achievement, and helps them to gain life skills and cope with everyday problems.

Case study 6.1 'Exclude me in' music project at Southampton YMCA

Overview

Alongside its tenants' representatives and other initiatives designed to increase the input, vision and ownership of service users, Southampton YMCA is pioneering 'Exclude me in', a multicultural project to engage excluded young people in the city.

The project works with people who have experienced direct or indirect exclusion from conventional learning, such as higher education, and are consequently unable to find a job or develop a career.

The project encourages regular tenants at Southampton YMCA to be involved in the running of the organisation, alongside its existing schemes such as tenants' meetings, consultations with staff and representatives, and opportunities for feedback.

Pilot project

With minimal help and oversight, the young people set up and ran the first project. They set themselves tasks, which they completed, provided evidence of their processes, and evaluated their tasks. At the end of the course, the staff gave the young people awards that recognised their achievements.

Through the project, the young people learnt how to write a CV, work as a team, look for a job, and developed confidence in themselves – skills they can continue to use in their everyday lives.

The project targets young people who do not have the confidence, self-esteem and determination to find and keep a job, join and stick with a training course, or play a full, active and positive role in their community. Because of this lack of self-belief the young people are encouraged, through the tasks, to develop individual and group confidence. This offers real benefits to them, the YMCA, and the wider community.

The young people who joined 'Exclude me in' in 2004 were totally transformed by the end of the course in 2005.

Eight young people took part:

- two young women and six young men
- aged 18 to 25
- six were white and two black Caribbean
- two were dyslexic.

Four young people completed the course:

- two young women and two young men
- aged 18 to 26
- four white
- none with special needs.

Achievements

Through 'Exclude me in' the young people:

- learnt to play the guitar
- learnt to read chords, and practise new chords without being shown
- improved their communication with the staff
- developed more patience. Some of the young people developed this skill quicker than others – and Eckersley reports that his patience increased too!
- learnt to encourage each other
- increased in confidence
- developed a sense of achievement, as they learnt something new
- developed a sense of worth
- built friendships with other participants.

The project was run in partnership with YMCA England, the national organisation that supports and develops the work of the YMCA, and the Youth Achievement Awards. Mark Hill, *aka* DJ Artful Dodger – who has worked with many high-profile performers, including Craig David – also offered his support. As well as endorsing the project, Emily Roberts, then Miss Southampton, presented awards to some of the participants – and this prompted her to become more involved in charity work involving music and young people.

TRANSITION TO INDEPENDENT LIVING

After living at a YMCA supported housing scheme, it is hard for some service users to make the transition to living in their own independent accommodation. Housing workers are there to make sure they do this at a time that is right for them. Through support and by listening to the young people, workers can inspire them with the confidence to live independently. At the right time, they can help the young people search for accommodation from council housing lists, find approved landlord schemes, make benefit claims and pay rent deposits. They can also help to find the furniture and other household items they need for living on their own.

It is a big step for a young person who has been in housing need to become self-sufficient and live independently. Taking control of their lives and where they live has great benefits for their future, and has a positive effect on the community. But transition is not always smooth. Without essential life skills, facing the world on your own is hard. Through participation in its programmes, the YMCA offers young people a real sense of self-esteem and confidence.

Putting a young person's individual needs first, the YMCA offers usable skills such as:

- budgeting
- personal hygiene
- cooking
- social skills.

First aid and general housekeeping

A sense of fun is an important part in the success of a programme, as it helps to create an atmosphere of 'shared learning'. For example, a course that helps the young people to make healthy choices in their diet will involve them in planning, budgeting, shopping for food, cooking and enjoying a meal together. Life skills programmes can also be made more enjoyable – and less like learning – by incorporating outdoor activity programmes or community arts projects, or through community work with people who are disabled or elderly.

Being inclusive – open to all – is the guiding principle at the heart of this work. At every stage, from planning to completion, the service users must be fully involved – to make sure the programme is designed to meet their needs.

Box 6.1 'My experience of service user involvement'

My role is to oversee all tenant user services. This involves issuing question-naires, holding tenant representatives' meetings and tenants' meetings, running training, social events and programmes. I am supported by the wider housing team who help with administration, induction, 'move on', re-ception and social elements – each member specialises in a specific area. Alongside the tenant participation officer, I plan how service users can get more involved.

I'm really pleased at how much more the tenants have become involved since I joined the management team. I came to the YMCA as a service user, so I know how negative the culture was in the housing sector from the late Eighties to the early Nineties. This was the time when the benefits of involving service users at high levels were first being championed.

At that time, many people doubted the value of service user involve-ment – some actively opposed it. I remember, when I was completing my housing diploma, there were many people working in housing that loathed the idea of working with or alongside tenants!

We are now reaping the many benefits of participation, thanks to the people who fought long and hard to implement programmes to make sure tenants were valued and involved. And, of course, because of the princi-ples of empowerment and shared ownership that come through participa-tion.

Southampton YMCA believes in the 'KISS' principle – 'keep it simple, stupid!' We hold monthly tenants' reps meetings, which helps to bring a sense of focus and order to our work and to the lives of the tenants who are involved. Many of our tenants came from difficult backgrounds and family environments.

Tenants' representatives are elected through a professional, demo-cratic process. We put out ballot boxes and distribute election papers to the tenants, who vote for candidates to be their representatives. When a rep leaves, the remaining reps nominate another tenant for the position. It is the policy at Southampton YMCA to apply a fully inclusive approach regarding black and minority ethnicity, asylum seekers and male/female ratios.

We've found food to be a great incentive to get young people to come along to tenants' rep meetings. We discuss the running of the centre over a takeaway curry or Chinese.

At the meetings, our aim is to build a sense of teamwork, vision and shared leadership. We encourage them to seek out and work with men-tors, observe and promote the rules – to lead by example to the other tenants.

We recognise that each tenant has special talents, so we give them responsibilities in these areas to exercise and develop their skills. These responsibilities include administration, food planning and preparation, and promoting and advertising of tenants' meetings and services. Through this, we nurture a sense of shared ownership. They are empowered to take control over areas of their lives.

Meetings are also a time for celebration, where we recognise achievements by individuals and groups – sometimes giving out gifts or awards.

Through all of this, we make sure that the reps take ownership of our tenant user involvement policy, which is overseen by the tenants' participation officer. The role of the officer is to develop the user involvement policy from the input and feedback of the reps. At Southampton YMCA, service users are involved with policy management and strategic development at all levels.

Terry Eckersley (n.d.)

Examples

Thanks to the input of its tenants' reps, Southampton YMCA significantly altered its emergency procedure and staff 'on call' policy. Similarly, through their involvement, it is considering a major redevelopment of its accommodation. The reps helped to construct a new application policy for people who wanted accommodation. Like all changes in policy, suggestions developed through involvement of the service users are considered for adoption by the board of management. Sometimes, tenants will be asked to make presentations at board meetings.

In other YMCAs, tenants sit on interview panels to help to select new staff – something that many at Southampton YMCA would like to adopt in future.

Southampton YMCA holds an annual review to assess all of its work, with the aim of creating in these meetings a positive atmosphere where all individuals can contribute.

BUDGETING

To demonstrate its commitment, Southampton YMCA allocates an amount in its budget to fund the involvement of service users. It shares this information with the tenants and reps to help nurture ownership and responsibility. The tenants' participation officer can request money from the involvement budget each month from the housing manager.

Projects funded so far include:

- inner-city housing collective five-a-side football tournament
- tenants' rep 'eat-out' consultations
- employing outside expertise for training courses
- purchasing music equipment and instruments and employing music teachers.

MULTICULTURALISM

The YMCA acknowledges and celebrates multiculturalism and holds regular nights to celebrate different cultures. At these events, its tenants cook dishes from their various countries, share music, national costumes and other aspects of their culture.

Again, Southampton YMCA has found that food and music offer a good incentive to get tenants to come along and participate. The multicultural evenings have proved to be a popular and successful part of life at Southampton YMCA – often more than three-quarters of its tenants participate. The multicultural evenings also prompted the idea of putting music at the heart of its 'Exclude me in' project.

Writer impressed by 'Exclude me in'

Richard Chorley is a freelance writer and artist who has run government-funded multicultural arts projects. He has produced short TV films in which popular actors have starred alongside previously untutored young people from BME communities. Richard also served on city council race consultative forums for the development of social cohesion policy and municipal equal opportunities sub-committees. In 2001 Meridian Television made a half-hour documentary, *Silent Soul*, which chronicled his work with aspiring actors and musicians from BME backgrounds.

Richard came along to the final presentation of 'Exclude me in', where tenants from many different cultures, communities and backgrounds came together for a night of performance and celebration. Impressed by the presentation and Southampton YMCA's multicultural programme, Richard said:

> I think if you go back a number of years, for those who cared, the single biggest worry in housing matters, as in all areas of life, was the exclusion of BME communities from decision-making processes. In a wide number of arenas, that definitely still persists today – but I think the route taken by Southampton YMCA is a potent one, the spirit of which could be transposed effectively into a lot of other organisations and public service circles.

Richard felt that, despite many advances, racial equality in Britain is still a subject that many people accept reluctantly. 'Far, far too many projects and associations are forced to accept and adopt equal opportunities programmes through legislation, rather than as a result of human engagement with the communities concerned', he said. 'Minimum quotas and ratios are met without a tangible change in the communal attitude and conduct of business in relation to these matters. While that remains the case, BME communities will continue feeling unwelcome inside the infrastructure of many areas of British life, and will not contribute to full potential levels. That is a massive, incalculable loss to the entire nation.'

In the current political and social climate, Richard believes that trends and developments underline his feeling that Britain still faces major problems of exclusion and conflict in the racial arena.

> It's as if the goalposts keep changing. With all the real and genuine advances made legally and socially in mind, the arrival of asylum seekers, as a major political issue of our times, shows us that that there is a deeply embedded culture of racism in Britain, which will still take many years of vision and work to erase. It is crucially important that we never forget that these levels of exclusion have been part of systematic racism that has blighted the lives and rights of whole sections of our society for centuries.

> What is important about the YMCA policy is its pragmatic celebration of BME origins and culture. The fact that people of varied origins gather and share elements culturally in a social environment where everybody feels relaxed and valued provides a springboard for future relations and progress. It is that *bona fide* sense of celebration, as opposed to legalised lip service, that has to be nurtured throughout society. If it is not, we will fail to see significant social advance in the first half of the new century.

TENANTS' MEETINGS

With the agenda set at the monthly reps' meetings, tenants' meetings take place on a set date each month – underlining the sense of order and focus established at the reps' meetings. Reps promote and encourage other tenants to come along to these meetings, which are characterised by a relaxed, friendly atmosphere.

Before the start of the meeting, the tenants play pool and mingle with each other while music plays in the background. The YMCA staff dress casually for the evening, and the first item on the agenda is the presentation of an award for the winner of the pool competition. Through these meetings the staff and tenants can break down barriers, build relationships and encourage each other.

The meetings continue the upbeat feel – celebrating achievements such as paying rent on time, and with rewards for other good behaviour. At the end, tenants are invited to raise any other business, such as issues and concerns about the running of the accommodation. Subjects that need more time will be added to the agenda of the next meeting. Through these meetings, tenants play a full and active role in the construction of Southampton YMCA's policies.

SOCIAL EVENTS

Part of the budget allocated to service users is used to fund social events and evening activities.

The focus of social events is fun, and they also promote unity. Again, food and music are used to encourage the tenants to come, and these social events are seen as a vital part of the life of Southampton YMCA. It is also a time when the residents and staff can build relationships and discuss issues in a relaxed setting – a friendly, fun environment. The events also have a purpose in that they help tenants with poor social skills to develop friendships and become more outgoing. These events follow the YMCA mission statement of developing people in 'mind, body and spirit'.

This is also an opportunity for Southampton YMCA to demonstrate how Christianity is the ethos behind its work, and demystify the often negative attitude people have to the faith. For people who want to look more deeply into the Christian faith, Southampton YMCA will direct them towards courses such as Alpha or Freedom in Christ. These courses aim to introduce the idea of a living, active faith that brings meaning, purpose and direction. Tenants' reps have been involved to coordinate and promote these courses – which also help to develop skills such as teamwork and leadership.

QUESTIONNAIRES

Southampton YMCA has found questionnaires to be a good way to encourage participation and to find out the opinions of its tenants, and questionnaires also help them to make new policies. Questionnaires are sent out each month and the items each covers are quite varied in order to achieve a good balance. The questionnaires are a good way to find out what tenants think about important issues, but they always include a fun element, with prizes and awards for creative contributions to tenant life.

TRAINING

In keeping with Southampton YMCA's belief in the input and participation of service users, it encourages them to help develop its training schemes. Tenant participation officers will find out from the tenants what training they think they need, and – alongside the housing staff and other agencies – work to construct appropriate courses.

One successful course that was developed in this way was the previously mentioned assertiveness programme, and a travel-planning course that resulted in a memorable trip to Prague. Through tenant participation and consultation, music training was added to the 'Exclude me in' programme.

EDUCATION

A partner of Southampton YMCA, UK Youth, exists to develop and promote innovative, non-formal education programmes for and with young people – working with them to develop their potential. Its three charitable objectives are: youth work development, networking and advocacy for youth work.

Youth work development

UK Youth focuses on the personal and social development of young people, and it believes that their potential is more likely to be maximised through non-formal education. It aims to apply the principles of effective youth work to the needs and interests of young people today through its accredited learning programmes.

It aims to work alongside government departments and agencies in the UK, Europe and beyond, and to promote coherent opportunities for and with young people. It also promotes these opportunities through partner agencies.

Networking

UK Youth believes strongly that to achieve its mission it must develop good relationships with organisations that share its beliefs and values. It supports its partnership networks by:

- promoting its youth work programmes to an increasing number of young people
- establishing and encouraging high standards and promoting common policies and approaches in the delivery of youth work

- supporting UK Youth members in the delivery of youth work programmes
- coordinating UK Youth members at a regional level to respond to political and legislative changes.

Advocacy for youth work

Directly, and with key partner organisations, UK Youth works to create an environment in which youth work is valued by promoting the social and economic benefits of high quality youth work, and it also publicises the distinct contribution that youth workers make. It focuses on:

- programmes developed by UK Youth
- perception of youth work
- policy development
- participation of young people.

Through its regional structure it provides training to staff and service users to run its programmes and promote the participation of young people.

Box 6.2 New York Housing – New England Corporate

The YMCA in the United States is facing similar pressure to the YMCA in England. In order to continue to receive tax cuts, the YMCA of the USA has to prove it is a Christian charity. It is interesting to see how far it has come from the origins of the YMCA where its three principles – symbolised by a red triangle – give equal importance to mind, body and spirit.

I visited many YMCA housing projects in New York where the Christian model of social care was exemplified. However, visiting colleagues and friends in the more affluent area of New England, the YMCA's core values were initially less identifiable in the gyms and fitness centres of corporate 'work-out' America. However, after talking to the staff it was clear that the YMCA's Christian ethos was still at the heart of its activities.

What my trip to America gave me was a firm sense of how traditional and contemporary practices were coming together as the YMCA continues to meet the challenges of the twenty-first century. My colleagues in New York and New England were very interested in the models and principles we are sharing in this book. This highlights the fact that we are at a very exciting time, on both sides of the Atlantic, for service user involvement, with both governments also encouraging growth in this area

Terry Eckersley (n.d.)

Workbook

Putting the basics in place

This section offers more details of Southampton YMCA's service user consultation processes and some tips for success. Following this, its service user consultation policy is reproduced – which was recently reviewed by the tenants' representative group, as part of their policy review.

Tenant participation officer

Ideally the participation officer should work full-time promoting user involvement with tenants. If your budget and structure do not allow this, you could add this as part of the role of a support worker. This can be effective, because you can rotate the role for 6- or 12-month periods among your staff. This will add to the team dynamics and skills base, with the emphasis on shared responsibility.

Budget

Allocating a budget for user involvement is very important as it enhances the credibility of the programme. By allocating funds you demonstrate that your organisation truly values and believes in the scheme. Service users also gain skills through working with a budget when planning and running a project.

Many organisations do not have a service user involvement budget. However, while it is true that most voluntary sector organisations are under great financial pressure, the value of offering funds to encourage participation of service users adds significantly to the development and sustainability of a project.

Tenant representatives

A tenant participation officer should work from the outset to create a representative group of tenants. It is also crucial to promote and create an election campaign with fliers and posters, and set up and monitor a ballot box.

Tenants should be involved at every step of the process. This is crucial to the group's initial development and for its long-term prospects. It is also important to motivate the tenants and encourage them to get excited about the process.

Once you have established a representative team, you can start allocating responsibilities to individuals. When you have identified their strengths and talents, you can allocate appropriate tasks. These may include: minute taking, preparation of food, buffet supervision at meetings, and general administrative duties. It is important to constantly encourage and promote a spirit of ownership and leadership within these roles and tasks. This will lead to further recruitment, and support from increased numbers of tenants for the group and its programme.

Try to make sure there is a training item on the agenda. This emphasises the continuing worth of the group by giving them new opportunities for personal growth.

Tenant representatives should be closely involved in development of new and existing policy, which helps to create a sense of involvement and consultation at all levels.

Keep all tenants, staff, management and board members constantly notified of meetings and significant developments inside the user programme. This will establish and maintain the profile of the group and actively encourage increased recruitment and future involvement.

Tenants' meetings

Tenants should be heavily involved in the planning, conducting and administration of meetings, which need to be varied and exciting. Elements of fun and challenge are essential in keeping interest levels high. The aim is not to let formal business features stifle the atmosphere, but to keep it fluid and inspiring.

A pre-meeting pool tournament is very popular at Southampton, with a trophy being presented at the start of each meeting. It is important to have a fun section on the agenda and to receive suggestions for social events and activities. A good tip is to always serve food at the end of meetings – serve it at the start, and many of the tenants will leave straight after!

Meetings need to be on a regular basis and officers must actively promote the meetings right up to when they start. A last-minute reminder may be all a resident needs to get them to come along.

Questionnaires

Questionnaires are a good first job for tenants' reps to work on. After creating an initial template, the participation officer could get the representatives to come up with ideas for what to ask other tenants about. When the participation officer identifies the reps' strengths, they can give each suitable individual responsibility for the design, delivery, collection and assessment.

Creative involvement

Southampton YMCA was given extensive help with its creative 'Exclude me in' project. It also received external accreditation from the youth achievement awards.

What creative talents does your organisation have that you can you tap into? What other partner organisations can help you be more creative?

The 'Exclude me in' concluding concert was a fantastic evening featuring celebrity judges like Mark 'The Artful Dodger' Hill, which demonstrated how much support we enjoyed from people in the music business.

When projects like 'Exclude me in' are developed, it is important not to limit the vision. Don't apply small parameters. Think big. It is always worth approaching local celebrities and business people. Many are actively looking for charitable projects they identify with to support. Often, all it takes is to pick up the phone. The support of a local celebrity or business leader will help enormously when promoting a project. Believe in yourself and what you are doing, and the world will too. Dream big dreams; take small steps.

We have included below our resident service user involvement policy as it was drafted by the residents and is reviewed by this changing group annually. We hope it may help others.

YMCA Resident Consultation Policy

1. Aims and Objectives

1.1 The YMCA aims to consult residents on all matters of housing management, maintenance and services where they are directly affected.

1.2 The purpose of consultation is to:

(a)   seek the views of residents on particular issues

(b)   enable residents to participate in the decision-making process

(c)   encourage residents to evaluate alternative solutions.

1.3 The Council of Management encourages staff to regard resident consultation as a rewarding experience rather than a necessary chore.

2. Responsibility for Action

2.1 The housing manager is responsible for ensuring the Management Committee's consultation policy is implemented. Whenever a consultation exercise is envisaged the director will follow the 'basic steps' outlined in Section 3. The process will be documented so that actions can be explained and the effectiveness of the process can be reviewed. The methods used and extent of the exercise will depend on the issue to be considered, the number of residents affected and the time available.

3. The basic steps

(a) Define clearly the issue or problem.

(b) Identify and investigate alternative options for action.

(c) Consult residents (see paragraphs 4.1 and 5.1).

(d) Implement the decisions taken.

(e) Review the process and effectiveness of the solution.

4. The consultation process

4.1 There are a number of key elements in the consultation process:

(a) The housing manager will ensure that all residents directly affected are consulted and given the chance to participate.

(b) Residents will be encouraged to consider a range of options.

(c) The housing manager will ensure that the decision taken takes into account the views of the majority of residents. The result should not reflect any domination by unrepresentative individuals or pressure groups.

(d) At the end of the exercise the housing manager will let all residents know the result of the consultation and explain how the decision will be implemented.

(e) Details of the process will be recorded by the housing manager.

4.2 In the following circumstances the consultation process may have to be curtailed:

(a) where the change or work is required as part of the landlord's statutory duty

(b) when health or safety factors mean immediate action is necessary

(c)   where no funds are likely to be available to resolve the issue within a reasonable timescale.

5. Methods available

5.1 The methods of consultation used will include:

(a)   letters

(b)   newsletters

(c)   questionnaires and resident satisfaction surveys

(d)   individual personal contact

(e)   residents' meetings

(f)   liaison with the residents' association.

5.2 The choice of method depends on the issue to be considered, the number of residents affected and the time available.

5.3 Residents' views will be made known to the Council of Management.

5.4 The YMCA will assist residents and the Residents' Association to obtain reasonable facilities for their own meetings.

6. Performance information for residents

6.1 The YMCA will make information available to residents relating to the following issues:

(a)   the charges made for different types of accommodation

(b)   rent collection performance

(c)   occupancy rates and a breakdown of the categories of people housed

(d)   vacant accommodation

(e)   repairs response times.

7. Complaints procedure and redress

See YMCA Complaints and Compensation policy. [Internal YMCA document, not included in this book]

CHAPTER 7

The Way Ahead

INTRODUCTION

This chapter summarises what we have covered in the book and looks at the way forward in the field of social housing.

From reading about the YMCA, the good practice examples, and more detailed case studies, we hope you now have more knowledge to help you reach any service users, but particularly those who are traditionally hard-to-reach, in an effective and mutually beneficial manner.

The case studies in particular offer a rich source of ideas for you to use or adapt, and also included in the book are three service user consultation policies: Worthing Churches Homless Project (Case study 3.2 in Chapter 3), the generic outline in Box 5.6 in Chapter 5, and the YMCA resident consultation policy in Chapter 6.

If you are a service provider and have followed the workbooks through alone or in a team, you will now have a comprehensive strategy for effective service user involvement for any client group you work with, and will be able to inform commissioners of your efforts and achievements.

As a commissioner of services for vulnerable people you should now have a clearer picture of how service users views' can be sought and put to good practical use at the strategic level for Supporting People, or any future or similar frameworks to come.

SO WHAT DOES USER INVOLVEMENT NEED?

Service user involvement needs planning, commitment, resources and the motivation of professionals to help erode real and perceived barriers faced by services users. Service user consultation can be organic in growth, and we have seen how vulnerable people can develop confidence and ability to participate in consultation processes, from basic daily decision-making in services, through to being trained to consult others and trained in strategic planning at the county level.

The following extract is taken from *The Hampshire Supporting People Strategy 2005–2010 Draft for Consultation* (Hampshire County Council 2005, pp.15–16) and was written by Graham Woods. This shows clear commitment to utilising service users' views at the highest level for strategic planning, through the two-tier model and by valuing the members of the Service User Reference Group (SURG) who consult with other service users in Supporting People services and feeding back the information. The draft was approved and is now in use. An excerpt follows:

Box 7.1 The Hampshire Supporting People Strategy 2005–2010

3.5 Communications

Following completion of the Year One activities and reviews, an updated coordinated Communication Strategy was required to ensure efficient information sharing with all partner agencies and interest groups. An updated structure has been developed incorporating levels of communication which are outlined below.

Level One sets out the communications structure proposed with strategic partners: health, housing, probation and social services.

Level Two sets out the communications structure proposed for Stakeholders including ROCC, the Provider Reference Group and SURG which together represent a variety of interested parties.

- **ROCC** (originally Resettlement of Offenders Coordinating Committee). Under Level Two of the Communications Strategy ROCC will be made aware of issues within the programme as they emerge.

- **The Provider Reference Group** meets quarterly to discuss topical operational issues, particularly relating to the review process and contracting. Current membership consists of a representative cross-section of Supporting People providers but all are welcome to attend.

- **SURG**. Chaired by ROCC, this body meets on a bi-monthly basis and focuses on consulting and developing Supporting People policy issues. SURG is the key strategic body for overseeing service user involvement processes in Hampshire. Membership is limited to ten users of Supporting People contracted services at any one time with every effort made to ensure that it is representative of all districts and

Supporting People Service User Groups. A member of SURG reports to the quarterly County Core Group (CCG) meetings giving service users an opportunity to express an opinion, in particular giving advice on policy development, consultation methods, and the quality of Supporting People services.

3.6 Involving service users

A key role for SURG members is to learn about important Supporting People issues, such as the review process and the commissioning of new services. Members then consult with their peers, feeding back the results to the next meeting and agreeing a policy or process proposal.

The consultation may be with: a tenant group, or those in a shared home, direct consultation with street homeless, to an established user, or via a wider survey. The key to SURG working effectively is to maintain a consistent membership throughout a year. This ensures members develop a good understanding of Supporting People and the current key issues.

Meetings are split into two half-day sessions; morning sessions normally include a presentation on a key policy issue (e.g. involving service users in the review process) from a member of the Hampshire Supporting People team. SURG members will then debate the issues and draw up a response, which is then taken back to their agreed consultation network, and brought back to the following meeting for final drafting. The final document submitted to the CCG has the 'SURG Approved' logo inserted across the top.

Training is provided during the second half of the day, aimed at developing participation skills such as constructing and giving presentations, minuting or chairing meetings.

Consultation

With a diverse range of client groups within the Supporting People programme, meaningful involvement of service users presents a considerable challenge. A 'one size fits all' approach cannot be adopted if a broad and robust user involvement programme is to be developed.

The Supporting People approach is to develop policy on consultation at all levels through SURG as set out above. All consultation is being undertaken across three key levels: strategic, service and personal.

Three levels of communications

Approaches to consultation

Supporting People wishes to encourage a broad methodology for obtaining a wide range of views. To achieve this, the use of primary methods of consultation will be encouraged – standard methods of information-seeking, such as one-to-one interviews, focus groups and questionnaires, and secondary methods where individual or group views are sought through more abstract approaches. These may include drama projects, art and design, theme days and special events.

As stated above, SURG are currently developing a broad policy on consultation in the review process. A draft document was submitted to the CCG in March 2005 setting out a consultation process that will include processes such as:

- SURG presentations to users at services due for review in a following quarter
- questionnaires covering all aspects of a service review
- a phone line for users to discuss issues relating to Supporting People.

Work started in April 2006 on developing policy on involving service users in the commissioning process.

Table 7.1 SURG achievements 2004

Policy area	Approach	Policy developed	CCG approval
Supporting People access to service user files	Consultation and discussion on access and confidentiality of support files	Access policy for Supporting People teams to service user files	October 2004
Hampshire Supporting People policy framework	Consultation with peers and discussion on implications of policy framework	SURG approved version agreed in final tier of consultation	Submitted to December meeting and approved
Consulting with service users in advance of service reviews	Develop a broad range of approaches to obtain service users' views on strategic relevance, quality, performance and value for money of services	Ongoing development of a policy for the Supporting People team to implement from April 2005	Submitted draft policy to the March 2005 meeting and approved

Hard-to-reach user groups

The Hampshire Supporting People team has been working closely with ROCC to develop a methodology for involving hard-to-reach people in the strategic decision-making of Supporting People. As well as providing an overall strategic response to engaging hard-to-reach groups this project has also produced good practice models for engaging views from hard-to-reach groups, including rough sleepers, night shelter users and young people in temporary accommodation.

The Hampshire Supporting People team has adopted the ROCC 'Guidance for Commissioners for Consulting with Hard-to-Reach Users' (Brafield 2003b) and uses it as a background document for all work through SURG on developing policy in this area. The full ROCC report can be found by going to the links below:

- Report – www.rocc.org.uk/publications/downloads
- Guidance – www.rocc.org.uk/publications/downloads

In 2006, ROCC finished helping a large local charity to develop a service user strategy utilising a ROCC consultant and service user from the Hampshire SURG who was paid for his essential contributions. This team worked over a six-month period to advertise for and gain a core group of service users, staff and a board member to act as a consultative group for the geographically dispersed charity. The role of the group was to find out from their peers what methods would work for them and compile a strategy that was core to the organisation but flexible enough for the different services. This was approved by the board and rolled out across the organisation.

In addition, ROCC have now sufficient funding to employ a member of staff to service the SURGs, as well as to further help member organisations develop quality work with their service users.

The three levels of consultation

Strategic level

This sets out how views are sought to better inform the planning and commissioning of services and how service user consultation can be used to better identify need and gaps analysis for new and existing services.

Service level

Supporting People teams have a requirement to involve at least 10 per cent of service users in the review process. Qualitative discussions are being held with service users as part of the service review process. Service users are able to tell the Supporting People team at validation visits, and shortly via stakeholder pre-review information, what they like or dislike about their service and what works and what does not.

Providers are required to provide evidence of their user involvement strategies and set out how their service users are involved at the service level.

Personal level

Service users must have the opportunity to express their views through a wide range of mechanisms, confidential and non-confidential, directly to the Supporting People team. Such mechanisms include confidential phone lines, mailboxes, email facilities, minority language formats, pictorial formats, and day-centre facilities, etc. Service users' support plans should also evidence a high degree of one-to-one consultation on the delivery of their support service. The Hampshire Supporting People whistleblowing policy is open to all users of contracted services.

LEVEL I STRATEGIC LEVEL

- SURG/POLICY AND CONSULTATION
- SUPPORTING PEOPLE TEAM STRATEGIC AND SERVICE REVIEWS

LEVEL 2 SERVICE LEVEL

- SURG PRESENTATIONS AND CONSULTATION
- SUPPORTING PEOPLE TEAM VALIDATION VISITS

LEVEL 3 PERSONAL LEVEL

- SURG CONSULTATION AND PHONE LINE
- SERVICE SUPPORT PLANNING
- SUPPORTING PEOPLE PHONE LINE

Figure 7.1 Three levels of consultation

THE WAY FORWARD

The following points may also be useful to remember when thinking about the development of service user involvement:

Size of organisation

Size does not matter! Potentially, smaller organisations and/or those with flatter hierarchies may be able to develop greater trust, rapport and involvement at all levels with less bureaucracy. Larger agencies with greater hierarchies may, however, have the capacity to set up internal groups, which could link to their higher-level decision-making body. In both cases, you can help service users to link with wider strategic groups such as SURG or other similar networks to inform commissioners making bigger picture policy.

Nature of consultation

It is crucial to ask service users how they would like to be consulted, and to be clear about how you will set up the processes, how they will work, what they are for, and what will happen to the information received. In addition, the outcomes will be fed back, so that service users feel that their views have been heard, respected and responded to.

Appropriate training and support should be offered where service users are consulting others on your behalf, and where more complex or strategic issues are concerned. One of the authors was at a meeting recently where a 'big cheese' suggested that service users would not be able to understand the finance issues, and his colleague reminded him how good service users can be on managing on the bare minimum of the benefits system!

The quality of a service offered may be perceived differently depending on whether clients feel they are giving their views as part of a customer satisfaction survey, or as part of a therapeutic intervention, when they may feel either more vulnerable or more trusting, depending on the circumstances. Within any group of people there will be some who are more able than others to make objective assessments, assimilate complex information and/or think strategically. As we have seen from service users themselves, they will have greater motivation and potentially greater ability when their personal circumstances are more stable than when they are not. So different methods may suit different people at different stages of their development and movement through services.

It is useful to offer choices of degrees of involvement in consultation processes so that people can take part in things that they are comfortable with, as well as be encouraged to stretch and grow to achieve their potential.

Having ensured that you have given these opportunities for training and/or taking part in consultation processes, you may still find, as with any group or population of people, that 5 per cent will be very happy with whatever you do, 5 per cent will be very unhappy with whatever you do, and of the remaining 80 per cent most will either be relatively happy or else not care either way!

Independence of service user views

It may be that each service user can only speak for themselves – for instance, as an individual homeless person, rather than as a representative of all homeless people. Discussions may need to take place about the perceived quality and quantity of service user views that would make a difference to a decision, within a service or at the strategic level for a county.

What the authors know is that the onus is on providers of housing-related support services to consult with their service users as a marker of enhanced quality provision under the Quality Assurance Framework, and only time will tell if this is an accurate measurement of service quality. As for commissioners, they could receive feedback directly from service users rather than going through the providers.

Balanced scorecard

This may be a useful model to look at in the future, as it can be used to assess progress or success in a business through its processes. As the voluntary sector has been under increasing pressure to become more businesslike, looking at performance management tools and adopting or adapting them is essential. Although under competing pressures from different funders for different data, organisations need to ensure that they can increasingly demonstrate value and quality for money.

In Helen Brafield's MBA thesis she compared two statutory bodies and two voluntary sector agencies, and found that they all had to become more professional in the following areas: strategy, governance, human resource management, and performance measurement (Brafield 2000).

So now, in the area of service user consultation, organisations and commissioners setting up service user consultation structures will need to find a way of measuring whether or not these are working effectively. This may involve assessing whether or not they are using the right method to ask the right questions to obtain the most appropriate feedback in response.

The principle of the balanced scorecard is that processes have outputs and outcomes, and that we can use these to obtain information essential to the vision and strategy of a business, in the areas of finance, internal business processes, learning and growth and the customer. An output is a measurable amount produced at the end of a process (generally quantitative data, how many or how much), whereas an outcome is the result or effect of a process (what happened, what improved) and is often more qualitative data.

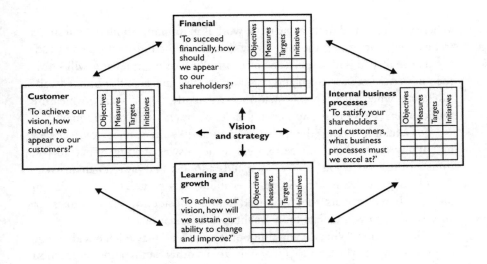

Figure 7.2 The balanced scorecard

This is not as complicated as it may appear! The authors have discussed many different methods and preferences for user consultation in this book – and it is often very clear what does not work, as people vote with their feet!

Within services, with the increased pressure to evidence practice, this is just another tool for your box. Look at a process, assess whether it meets the need, i.e. provides the outcome or output that is useful, and log it. Through actively reviewing processes, you will be demonstrating commitment to continuous improvement (always seen as a good thing by most funders), as well as ensuring that you are using the most effective method to obtain the information you need.

You can obtain quantitative and qualitative data from a process such as consulting SURG, for example, in year one. You could define the outputs as, for example:

- six meetings were held
- 60 service users were consulted between times
- four documents were written or amended.

Outcomes may be that service users:

- contributed revisions to documents
- made significant contributions to the five-year strategy
- reported that their confidence increased.

Where you may need to do some more work is in thinking about the questions to be asked, and asking them in a way that elicits the information you need.

Those of you with experience of counselling or interviewing will know the difference between open and closed questions, and such things need consideration when eliciting information, particularly if you want to measure service users' views in groups, or in greater numbers using questionnaires.

For example, asking the question 'Do you like the service you receive?' potentially closes the response to a yes or no answer. Asking 'What do you think of the service you receive?' demands a longer and more open answer.

Although there is great value in enabling service users to help design question-based formats, they will need help in considering the usefulness of answers and how to collate more qualitative information.

The question 'What do you think of the service?' may elicit a wide range of answers that can be hard to pin down. On the other hand, rating satisfaction with frequency of keyworker contact or feeling safe in your premises may provide more measurable answers from which to build evidence. Scales of 'not very happy' to 'very happy' will give an overall feel for a service, and can lead to questions such as 'What improvements would you like to see?' for you to consider.

THE WAY AHEAD

It is the authors' intention that this book helps to clarify the benefits of inclusive service user participation in consultation at all levels from day to day, through service development and staff recruitment and training, to

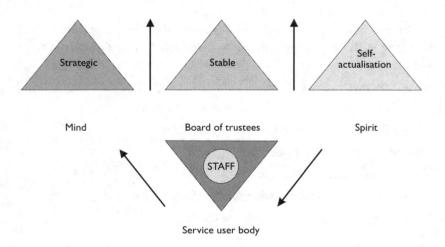

Figure 7.3 Brafield and Eckersley's Pyramids of Involvement

independent models to inform commissioners at the strategic level of service design and delivery.

Through writing this book, we have developed a 'pyramids of involvement' model, where progress upwards on the first three pyramids, combined with two-way communication in the lower one, enables service users to realise their potential, with support, where needed, for further development. In addition senior planners can be aware of the issues facing users of housing-related support services and ensure that they keep communication flowing.

It is clear to us and those taking part in effective service user consultation that you have to work with any perceived barriers to break them down, and develop a culture across the sector that genuinely respects and consistently engages with service users. Figure 7.4 below shows how central service users' views should be to ensure the ongoing success of an organisation.

It is also important where there are pockets of good practice that these are shared so that others can benefit and learn.

As history has dictated and we have learned: by being human, cutting through jargon and offering genuine choices, we can empower service users to be as involved as they wish in the continuous improvement of the housing-related services they receive, through consultation and involvement.

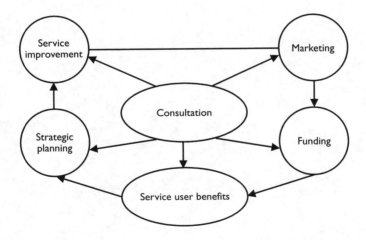

Figure 7.4 Service user benefits

CHAPTER 8

Devising Your Own Consultation Strategy

INTRODUCTION

This chapter discusses a range of practical techniques to help you devise your own consultation strategy.

- Part 1 looks at how to manage the costs and offers a good practice example.
- Part 2 offers a detailed report from a successful conference involving service users.
- Part 3 provides an overview of project management techniques, which you may find useful.

The workbook at the end of this chapter will help you to complete the process of devising your own comprehensive strategy for service user involvement, including policy, procedures and methods.

PART 1: HOW TO MANAGE YOUR COSTS

Cost is one of the barriers commonly cited as preventing service user involvement in consultation exercises. However, as we have seen in this book, consultation about a variety of issues can happen during the daily interaction between client and service provider. Even those people who would fall into the hard-to-reach categories engage, at some time, with a Supporting People service and receive keywork sessions.

All keywork sessions could therefore include a discussion of how the service will help the individual achieve their goals, and also gather their views on the service received to date – whether it meets their needs, what could be improved, etc.

If your service develops a culture of asking service users for their views and responding positively wherever possible to their suggestions, then your users may be more inclined and able to contribute to stand-alone consultation events, for which you could offer some payment or reward.

When setting budgets, it is important to remember to incorporate a specific budget for user consultation activities. Supporting People is all about empowering individuals, and support time can be well spent in user consultation exercises.

For example, the Southampton YMCA spends approximately £150 per month on activities promoting service user consultation, and this has in turn built the required momentum to set a positive culture of inclusion for current and new tenants.

Included on the agenda have been upbeat items – for example, enabling tenants to plan and execute social activities together. These upbeat items help to avoid the tendency towards 'moaning cycles' and encourage better working relationships. In turn, this approach promotes involvement in the less interesting activities where you need service users' views, such as policy review.

The following case study looks at how the Advance Housing Association has set up service user focus groups in order to better consult with them as part of an inclusion unit. It also shows how users offered their views on how they would like to be consulted, and how they contributed directly to policy development. Again, the presence of a motivated and dedicated member of staff has added to the success of this venture.

Case study 8.1 Advance Housing Association
Background

The Advance Housing Association (AHA) currently has two service user focus groups. The association set up the groups in March 2004 after the newly formed 'inclusion unit' carried out an audit to identify the association's current status in terms of community involvement and tenant and service user participation. AHA is a large organisation covering 26 counties and there are only three staff in the inclusion unit, who do not always get to hear about all of the good practice across the organisation!

The inclusion unit consists of: inclusion manager, tenant and service user participation officer and community involvement officer.

Questionnaires were sent out by the inclusion unit to all tenants, service users and support staff at AHA. Part of the purpose of the questionnaires was to explain who was involved and how they would be involved, including the role of unit staff.

One of the questions asked was if service users would be interested in being involved in the inclusion unit's activities, and quite a few said they would be.

From this, the team has set up two focus groups, one in the South, consisting of about eight people with a learning disability, and the other in the Midlands, consisting of seven people with a mental health problem. AHA would obviously like to set up more groups. They rely heavily on staff support so that people can get to meetings, and this is not always easy!

Since March 2005, the focus groups have been involved in the consultation process on some new policies and are rewriting some old ones. The participation officer and community involvement officer have facilitated these meetings, enabling people to give their ideas and opinions, which are then fed back.

The focus groups have recently been involved in a big exercise examining how AHA can communicate more effectively with the people they support (accessible communication). The groups were able to offer a lot of input into this project, particularly about their own preferences for communication methods!

Some members of the group are also involved in producing a new Support and Homes File, which people receive when they become AHA tenants and/or service users. The focus group members are working with AHA 's quality department to identify the information new tenants and service users need.

AHA would like to expand the groups, and hopes to do so in 2006. They are also exploring ways of involving people with more complex needs, and will be working with staff to support this.

(Case study prepared from information kindly supplied by Sharon Picken, community involvement officer.)

Service providers

Managers need to respect the relevance of asking service users to inform all aspects of their service delivered under Supporting People, and to communicate this clearly to their staff and service users. Managers also need to ensure that their staff are fully aware of the different methods they could use with little or no cash cost, and that involving people in consultation exercises is a valid method of promoting service users' independent living skills.

Support workers

In the main, the authors have observed support workers tasked by their managers to attend training on service user involvement. They have generally been keen to engage with service users in consultation processes, but felt unclear about what to do and how to measure it.

Often staff had thought primarily in terms of needing to get everyone together according to a traditional model of a conference or 'away day', thus incurring costs in terms of time, transport, childcare, etc. It must be stressed that this is not always necessary and that staff can make use of their daily contact with service users to build rapport and engage them in open discussions about the services they receive.

Additionally, a lot of supported housing services have natural gatherings such as mealtimes or house meetings, where they can seek views on not just the day-to-day issues, but also the longer-term issues, such as staff recruitment and training, policy and procedure discussions and development.

Often policy issues can appear dry and dull to staff as well as service users, so again it is up to staff to present these in an interesting and stimulating way. If this achieves nothing else, it gives service users some authority in decision-making and greater clarity and understanding about the framework within which services have to operate, such as health and safety or protection from abuse.

Commissioners

The Service User Reference Groups (SURG) for Supporting People for Hampshire and Portsmouth saw that there was a cost to providing a room, refreshments, facilitator, administration, travel and payments for service users. We must, however, weigh this against the benefits of setting up a stable core group and an ever-widening network of service users happy to speak to the core members. This information-seeking is truly independent of service providers, although they can enable greater access to the core group members as they expand the network over time.

For Portsmouth and Hampshire the rewards have been invaluable. As Supporting People teams can demonstrate, they have consulted and responded positively to the feedback of service users.

Payment and reward for service users

There are consequences to making cash payments to service users claiming a variety of benefits, so the authors would recommend large one-off payments that only affect one week's benefit (for example, as payment for contributions made over a period of time that can be specified), so that no more than, say, £5.00 per hour for four hours is earned, which keeps most people within the earnings limit. Alternatively you can give vouchers for specific shops.

When we consult service users, we find that it is not often the cash value and potential hassle this involves that is important – rather, the non-monetary rewards gained through an individual's participation. It is always worth asking service users how they would like to be rewarded: many want to improve their personal skills, gain confidence, and obtain a reference from a recognised source citing their contributions. A good example of this is in Southampton YMCA, where tenant consultation meetings provide food chosen by service users and bought out of the allocated budget. This always guarantees a high turnout and individuals like the opportunity to choose different meals, such as buffets or Chinese or Indian food, contributing a wider multicultural aspect to the sessions.

Box 8.1 Summary of benefits and earnings allowances – current rules in 2006/07

The following means-tested benefits can only work 16 hours a week or less.

- **Job Seekers Allowance** (single person) – can only earn £5 per week, or will lose £1 benefit for each £1 earned.

- **Income Support** – depends on length of time of claim and reason for claim.

- Generally:
  - A single person can only earn £5 per week and will lose £1 benefit for each £1 earned over this.
  - A couple can only earn £10 per week and will lose £1 benefit for each £1 earned over this.
  - A lone parent can only earn £20 per week and will lose £1 benefit for each £1 earned over this.
  - A carer can only earn £20 per week and will lose £1 benefit for each £1 earned over this.
  - If a person on a disability premium such as Disability Living Allowance, or has been claiming sickness benefit for over one year, they can also earn £20 per week and will lose £1 benefit for each £1 earned above that.

- Incapacity benefit
  - If solely claiming this, can do permitted work to earn up to £20 per week, the lower limit.
  - If earning more than £20 per week, it is more complex and there are time restrictions.
  - If on Incapacity Benefit and Income Support, the Income Support rules count.

The Benefits Office only encourages work valued at minimum wage or above, i.e. £5 per hour or more. This means that someone could work four hours in any given week for a user involvement project. Travel expenses and childcare expenses are not included in benefits assessments and will not affect benefits.

Please note that these are general rules only, and it is recommended that each person should go to their own paying office for advice specific to their benefit or combination of benefits and to tell them details of their work, hours and payments. Be sure to get the most up-to-date benefits advice from your local benefits agency regarding the blanket regulations and how these affect an individual's benefits package, as these are updated annually.

Community or treasure chest

Another method you could use to acknowledge users' involvement is for the organisation to make a payment into a 'community or treasure chest', which would then be used to provide additional activities or services for users, such as training, social events, or perhaps payments to individuals to help them move into employment or live independently. (As mentioned earlier, this suggestion came from a ROCC workshop on involving mental health service users in the design, delivery and evaluation of training.)

Such a fund could potentially serve all groups of service users and cover both statutory and voluntary/independent agencies. At first, the fund might simply benefit those individual service users who had put time, effort and commitment into the consultation and involvement process. In time, however, you could develop it to benefit the wider population of users. The fund could also move beyond making payments or grants to individuals, and develop as a 'micro-credit' scheme offering low- or no-interest loans to members of the community who might otherwise be unable to access credit at reasonable cost.

PART 2: 'GETTING BETTER?' – A SUCCESSFUL CONFERENCE

This good practice example demonstrates how an organisation can effectively consult people who misuse substances by asking them to attend a conference.

Initially the authors were going to summarise the following report, but on reflection decided to reproduce it in full. It is an excellent example of service users being consulted with, to contribute towards the continuous improvement of drug services in their area.

Key points from the good practice example:

- You need to be proactive with non-substance misuse agencies, so that they understand the needs of your group and can participate in initiatives and cooperative working.

- Satisfaction forms were handed out as people were leaving. This allows people to sum up the day's events (but it's best to get them before they leave the venue or you may never get them back!).

- Ex-service users should have more involvement in the services. Mentoring and peer support schemes can help service users make this transition.

- Service users feel that the assessment process is beneficial if it involves discussion and agreement with them.

- Service-led assessments that are inflexible and not based on user needs are seen as creating barriers and reducing choice.

- Service reviews need to include clients.

- Daycare does not always provide the same opportunities for consultation as time and recovery progresses. Some service users would like more time for individual counselling sessions.

- Keyworkers should be positive people!

- User involvement is the key for the success of any of these projects.

- There should be more dialogue between the service users, drug teams and GPs, as GP involvement is often minimal.

- Organisations have to make sure that service users know what the organisation is doing, so that they can access the services and comment upon them.

- There are still several issues to resolve, but 'things will get better much quicker if we all work together' – this was the key message of the conference.

The report published following the conference held in February 2004 provides useful information in the following areas:

- reason for holding the conference
- formats of the conference
- numbers of participants
- views of service users
- actions to be taken.

The report shows that, although a conference may be a more traditional method of consultation for this hard-to-reach service user group, if you plan and manage it well it can be a very positive and inclusive event.

'Getting Better?' – improving substance misuse services: the conference report

The target audience included service users, carers and practitioners and other agency staff in Cornwall, and the Isles of Scilly Drug and Alcohol Action Team (DAAT).

1. What was it?

The idea for the first annual 'Getting Better?' conference arose out of a desire among certain service users, drug workers and the DAAT to consult a wide number of people on what needed to be done to improve services, not because existing services were seen to be poor, but because it was felt that there is always room for improvement.

Following an 'Opening Doors to Treatment' conference in Stoke-on-Trent, organised by the National Treatment Agency in 2003, the team that attended this event established the 'Getting Better?' conference team.

The team began by mapping treatment pathways, setting out the various stages in a client's journey through treatment to recovery. These stages then formed the basic structure for the conference, and the team agreed a workshop format that would enable delegates to consider the following questions.

1. What is good about our current services? What can we build on?

2. What is not so good about our services? What do we need to change?

3. What can we do to improve our services?

Twelve different workshops focused on:

- finding out
- being referred
- being accepted
- having an assessment
- the care plan
- counselling
- substitute prescription
- daycare
- care coordination
- detox and rehab
- reviews
- aftercare and resettlement.

By using morning and afternoon sessions, delegates were able to attend two workshops of their choice. The facilitators were two volunteers drawn from service users, practitioners and managers.

Each workshop spent 15 minutes identifying the positives, 15 minutes on the negatives and 30 minutes on suggestions for improvement within its allocated topic. The facilitators recorded notes on flipcharts, identifying three key points against each question. Delegates also completed a feedback sheet to record their personal views so that these could be included in the consultation.

2. What was it for?

The agreed conference objectives were:

- to consult as wide a range of stakeholders as possible, on the three questions listed above
- to ensure that service users and carers would participate on an equal footing with practitioners and planners
- to promote a better understanding of the models of care guidance, and strengthen inter-agency relationships
- to begin to engage Tier 1 agencies (e.g. social services, housing, probation) more fully with substance misuse treatment services
- to provide the DAAT with an opportunity to consider its annual plan against a background of stakeholder expectation.

3. Who was there?

Table 8.1 Details of the delegates

Agencies, etc.	Numbers attending	
	Professional	Clients
Al Anon	3	
Bosence	7	14
Cornwall and District Addaction	10	6
Carer	3	
Community Drug Action Team	17	37
Citizens Advice	0	
Freshfield Service	5	
Gwellheans	4	10
Housing Advice	0	
Narcotics Anonymous	0	
New Connections	1	1
National Treatment Agency	1	0
Pentreath Industries	2	
Probation	2	
Stonham	8	
St Petroc's	3	0
Supported Housing	1	
Youth Service	1	
Total delegates	68	68

4. How were people's views recorded?

Each workshop produced flipchart notes of the key issues, and delegates were provided with feedback forms.

Table 8.2 Individual feedback forms

Workshop title	Number of feedback forms
Finding out	5
Being referred	7
Being accepted	8
Having an assessment	7
The care plan	4
Counselling	3
Substitute prescription	5
Daycare	9
Care coordination	8
Detox and rehab	12
Reviews	5
Aftercare and resettlement	15
Conference satisfaction forms	27

Table 8.3 Satisfaction survey

Conference satisfaction questions	Yes	No
Did the conference fulfil your expectations?	26	1
Did you have the opportunity to put your ideas across?	25	2
Did you find the conference useful?	27	0
Was the venue easy to find?	25	2
Did you feel well looked after?	27	0

5. What were the issues raised?

Geography: There is a problem about transport, access to, provision and knowledge of services across the county, with a consensus of opinion that north and east Cornwall do not have parity of provision.

GPs: These were criticised by nearly all the groups as generally ill-informed about addictions and relevant services, and for being reluctant to provide or refer for treatment. This presented the service user with difficulties in getting a diagnosis or finding out where to go for help. In addition, when in treatment, many of the groups noted that GPs are not kept informed (or given accurate information) about their patient's progress.

One stop shop: There was general agreement that, a 'one stop shop' for initial contact, 'triage' and signposting would be very helpful. This would need widespread publicity and inter-agency cooperation, but would reduce confusion and delay while providing equality for referral and access to services. Another suggestion was for multi-agency working under a single coordinator. The suggestion is to 'keep it simple'. (Why do service users need to get to rock bottom before they can get help?)

Helpline: Many of the participants suggested that, although the National Drug and Alcohol Helplines are useful, a 24-hour free helpline could be set up in Cornwall to provide information and crisis support. Information about the agencies and available services could be through a newsletter. This service could be advertised through doctor's surgeries, Citizens' Advice Bureaux and drop-in facilities.

Resources: It was felt that there was a lack of resources and facilities for young people and that more attention should be focused on education and harm reduction.

Media: Attention was given to the press reports and media coverage that associates addiction negatively with crime, disorder and antisocial behaviour. Delegates suggested that positive editorials and publicity could raise awareness and help to educate the general public about the wider issues.

User involvement: Many people thought it would be helpful for ex-service users to have more involvement in the services, although some thought there was risk if service users became staff too soon. Schemes involving service users mentoring each other and peer support were suggested as beneficial. An autonomous self-help facility, run by service users for service users but working with other agencies, was suggested as a way forward. Another suggestion was a men's group with a men's leaflet. Support and action should be encouraged at a local level.

Venues: There should be more dedicated, appropriate venues for drop-in and support groups. These could be available in the evenings and at weekends when service users feel particularly vulnerable, providing a place to build confidence and socialise, which could be ongoing. There was widespread concern that the out-of-hours services were poor, especially for those not engaged with Alcoholics Anonymous or Narcotics Anonymous. This needs to be combined with greater support for families and carers.

Inter-agency cooperation: This was seen as another key issue, with rivalry between the agencies fuelled by funding problems causing lack of feedback on referrals, lack of flexibility, choice, coordination, continuity and communication.

Forums and seminars: The opportunities for client participation forums and seminars are particularly welcomed.

Supported housing schemes: Where these are available, the feedback was extremely positive, but it is clear that these vital services are rationed and scarce, and more would be appreciated. Along with the employment of resettlement/aftercare workers, there is a need for assertive, flexible outreach workers to provide ongoing encouragement, advice and support. It seems, for some, that the transition from detox to independence is too abrupt and there is little help (e.g. links with flexible and accessible drop-in facilities) available at times of difficulty and stress.

For those coming out of prison, suitable affordable housing seems impossible to attain. Some delegates felt stranded in hostel accommodation following discharge from detox/prison/rehab. There are many problems for the homeless in accessing help and treatment, as they often do not have a contact address for appointments.

Detox beds: Another area of concern was the lack of detox beds for both alcohol and drug users in Cornwall, causing difficulties in accessing them, delays and waiting lists. Home detox for drug users was viewed positively. The provision of detox beds in the county was viewed as a priority by many.

Response times: Delays in getting assessment and treatment were seen as major difficulties and it was hoped that a more rapid response to assessment and accessing services might be implemented.

'Crisis' house: There is a need for a crisis house where people can go for help and support when they are not clean/dry.

There should be a chance to return to services after disengagement.

Specific issues: There was general criticism of 'paperwork', 'procedures' and 'red tape', and also of lack of choice concerning keyworkers.

Pre-assessment: Pre-assessment is regarded as a helpful opportunity to talk through the available options and methods in a safe, confidential and trusting environment, and to explore service user expectations before any paperwork or commitment is entered. Physical and mental health needs can be addressed.

Assessment: The benefits of the assessment process were itemised as follows.

- Confirmation of start of treatment process: the service user feels that they are being taken seriously.
- The assessment is relevant and the service user is treated with respect and they individual needs are being heard and addressed.
- The assessment is confidential, conducted in private, and the service user realises they is not alone and sets the pace.
- The process may take more than one session and immediate support may be needed while the process continues.
- The assessment involves discussion and agreement with the service user.
- With an integrated assessment there should be less repetition and delay.
- Assessors need to be open and honest about what is available, so that service users can make informed choices.
- Assessment is an ongoing process and needs updating, and to be carried out in changing contexts.
- A comfortable, private and suitable venue was seen as important.
- There should be the opportunity for the person being assessed to bring a friend or advocate with them. This should be written in the letter of invitation to the assessment and a copy sent to the referrer.

The problems with assessment were identified as follows.

- The common assessment causes confusion as the different agencies have different perspectives and needs.
- The assessment is often done long after immediate help has been requested.
- Poor assessments result from referrals couched in prejudicial terms, and from lack of good communication between the referrer and the practitioner, or where the practitioner is patronising or negative.
- Social services were seen as threatening and rude in their responses to people with addictions.

- Service-led assessments are inflexible and not based on user needs, and are seen as creating barriers and reducing choice.
- If time lags are too great, the potential service user abandons hope and gives up before treatment starts.
- Service users may feel the need to exaggerate in order to secure service.
- If the assessment process is too rigid, it may be difficult to make users 'fit' the existing framework.
- From the providers' perspective, assessment in a neutral place may mean they do not see the service user in context.
- How do service providers cope with users with unrealistic expectations?

Care plans, reviews, counselling and daycare: The services provided need to be holistic, taking account of physical, mental, emotional and spiritual needs.

Care plans:

- It appears that these are most valuable for continuity and as a guide.
- They are not always discussed and agreed with the service users, it is not always clear who is coordinating care when it is shared among various agencies, and not all participants always get a copy of documentation. Shared care is wonderful when it works, but sometimes continuity is lacking.
- Care plans are not always client-focused.
- The document should be confidential to the relevant parties, and those involved treated with respect.
- It seems there have been problems for service users in getting the care plans amended when their circumstances change, or in challenging a care plan.
- Not enough attention is given to exit strategies when care plans are drawn up.
- There should be clear follow-up links after detox/discharge.

Reviews:

- Reviews are not always regular and timely.
- Reviews were often not well attended by the significant players. Sometimes clients were not included in the review.

- Reviews are good for recognising and acknowledging progress.
- They can be a useful 'to do' list.
- At times they can be used in punitive way.

Counselling and daycare:

- Counselling is generally welcomed as a person-centred approach to problems. However, there was debate about how well trained and qualified some of the counsellors are.
- The need for more emphasis on 'real' issues was highlighted.
- There are problems for those with dual diagnosis in accessing services, and it was suggested that better links were needed.
- One-to-one counselling, which is not time-limited, allowing trust to develop, in addition to therapeutic groups, can be helpful, providing a range and choice of service.
- How the services are accredited and how quality is assured were two of the questions raised.
- Daycare is seen as offering structured activity, with a chance to learn new skills or useful training including how to socialise.
- Daycare provides a return to normality, with peer support as a motivating force.
- Daycare provides access to information and advice, particularly on practical issues such as housing and benefits, and can be fun.
- The problems are that some find it too structured
- Lack of funding means that there is not enough and availability is not evenly distributed throughout the county.
- One suggestion to remedy the availability was a mobile unit.
- Childcare, transport, access and inflexible hours are other reasons why people cannot always easily make use of the facility.
- There are not always the same opportunities to be listened to as time and recovery progress. Some would like more time for individual counselling sessions while engaged with daycare.
- Keyworkers should be positive people.
- There was a desire expressed for more workplace schemes (progress to work scheme is seen as good) to be made available, and for additional assertive outreach work.

- There seems to be a gap in service provision between detox and daycare; it was suggested that use of other generic services could be explored.

- User involvement is the key for the success of any of these projects.

- Although there was widespread support for the back-to-work scheme, concern was expressed that the original daycare scheme was changing and no longer felt so welcoming or a safe haven, and fares are now only paid to attend accredited courses. An extension of the original service in other areas around the county would be the preferred option, so that support and advice could be readily accessible without the need to travel long distances as well as the work and training schemes.

Substitute prescribing:

- Substitute prescribing has many positive attributes. It takes away the chaotic lifestyle associated with drug addiction, is healthier and less risky, and there is no need for further dangerous criminal activity.

- It is viewed as the start of help and part of treatment and access to further holistic care.

- The pace is set by the service user with no time limits, but opportunities for change are available.

- There is a good range of prescribing treatments in Cornwall.

The difficulties are:

- It is not easy to get an initial referral/assessment. The processes need to be speeded up; it would be better if there were no waiting list.

- The system is open to abuse, staff can be manipulated, and there could be leakage.

- There can be issues of control.

- There are concerns about the primary care trusts' commitment to continue to fund treatment.

- There is difficulty for some in accessing pharmacies to pick up prescriptions, and no privacy for consumption, which some service users find degrading.

- There could/should be more dialogue between the service users, drug teams and GPs, as GP involvement is often minimal.

- Sometimes other problems are not addressed.
- Attention could be given to further research and drug treatment as an option for alcohol addiction.
- More listening time is neeeded as treatment progresses.
- The telephone link with CDAT (Community Drug Action Team) is not consistent

6. To what extent were the conference objectives achieved?

- *To consult as wide a range of stakeholders as possible*: partially met. Specialist drug and alcohol agencies, and services users in particular, were well represented. More could have been done to attract non-specialist agencies.

- *To ensure that service users and carers would participate on an equal footing with practitioners and planners*: met. Fifty per cent of delegates were service users and carers. Feedback identified the value of facilitated groups, and a large number of workshop forms were handed in with the flipchart notes. Many service users commented that they felt valued, that there was no 'them and us' atmosphere, and that they were treated as equals with the professionals.

- *To promote a better understanding of the models of care guidance and strengthen inter-agency relationships*: met. Delegates reported a desire for multi-disciplinary teams, agencies working together, and there was recognition of the importance of integrated care plans.

- *To begin to engage Tier 1 (e.g. social services, housing, and probation) more fully with substance misuse treatment services*: not met. With the exception of probation and mental health, Tier 1 services did not attend.

- *To provide the DAAT with an opportunity to consider its annual plan against a background of stakeholder expectation*: met. Conference feedback appears to support elements of the annual treatment plan and has influenced service planning and development.

7. What happens next?

First of all, the way we do things now has to be examined in the light of the issues raised at the conference, and our plans will need to take account of this. The DAAT and the service providers will need to explain to our stakeholders what is being done to improve services, and services will need to be regularly reviewed to ensure that these improvements actually work.

Review

The conference was itself part of a review process, which looks at whether or not services do what they say they do, do what is needed, and are effective. Reviews include monitoring of DAAT plans and processes by government agencies; monitoring of DAAT activity by local health, social care and community agencies; local service monitoring by the DAAT and service providers; and stakeholder consultation through service user meetings, inter-agency forums and conferences.

Planning

The DAAT produces an annual plan covering all aspects of drug and alcohol service in Cornwall and the Isles of Scilly (Cornwall County Council DAAT 2005). This can be viewed on the DAAT website at www.cornwall.gov.uk on the Health and Social Care page. The plan is prepared during the winter for implementation in the next financial year, and has to be approved by national and local government agencies. The plan will show what will be done to address the issues identified in reviews, including the conference feedback.

Doing

Action, not talk, is what most people want, and we need to make sure that we do what we set out to do in the plan. We record what we achieve, what we cannot achieve, and identify the gaps. We have to make sure that people know what we are doing so that they can access the services and comment upon them.

The cycle

If we do all of these things, we should get better. However, it can be uphill work, especially if people are working on their own. Things will get better much quicker if we all work together, which is what the conference told us! Overall, feelings about this conference were very positive and the day was both productive and fun.

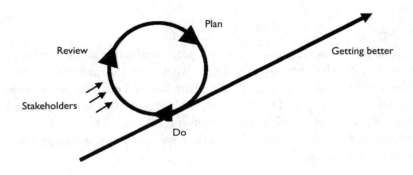

Figure 8.1 Stakeholder consultation cycle

PART 3: THE PROJECT MANAGEMENT PROCESS
Introduction

This part of the chapter provides an overview of project management techniques, which you may find useful. You can either read through the whole section or 'pick and mix' from the techniques suggested.

- What is project management and why is it useful?
- What skills does a project manager need?
- The project management process:
    - scoping
    - planning
    - implementation
    - evaluation.

What is project management and why is it useful?

The concept of project management has been used and developed predominantly in the engineering, building and IT industries in order to plan and implement complex projects, so that the necessary tasks happen in the right order, and the finished product meets deadlines and targets regarding the cost, quality and timescale set for the project.

In order for you to focus on achieving a service user consultation and involvement strategy for any client group at any level, we suggest that you make use of some project management tools.

Project management tools are suitable when you need to carry out a piece of work involving a team of people that has an obvious end point.

For a service user consultation strategy, there may be finite goals such as the production of a written strategy or policy, but once this is achieved and the 'project' has been completed you may wish to review it at intervals afterwards, on the basis that this is a topic with many variables, and that you and your service users are unique individuals working in an ever-changing environment.

What skills does a project manager need?

As the project manager you will need to be skilled in:

- communication
- facilitation, to interface with the team and the client or sponsor
- time management
- influencing
- teambuilding
- problem solving
- decision-making.

Oh, and enthusiasm, belief, and a sense of humour coupled with a certain resilience when under stress are also invaluable attributes!

The project management planning process

It may be useful to start by using a project management planning process which has four phases:

1. **Scoping**: start by setting objectives gleaned from ideas, problems and issues discussed.

2. **Planning**: plan and schedule time and costs, looking at the feasibility of the objectives, and planning everything that you reasonably can.

3. **Implementation**: implement the plan by carrying out agreed actions to the specified outcomes.

4. **Evaluation**: evaluate the results of the project in terms of what worked and didn't, including lessons learned.

Scoping

This is the process whereby you decide what the project will achieve and set objectives to enable this to be realised. You may like to use these two methods as groundwork:

1. SWOT analysis, which looks at the Strengths, Weaknesses, Opportunities and Threats of, and to, your current position [in terms of service user involvement].

2. SMART objectives i.e. those that are Specific, Measurable, Achievable, Realistic and Time-limited.

In order to do this it is important that you have a team to help carry out the work. It is likely to be made up of staff, and hopefully some service users. It is important that the team feels valued and respected and that communication is very clear concerning their roles and responsibilities and deadlines for tasks to be achieved.

The framework for the team should include these points, as well as looking at how you will recognise contributions and how the team will monitor its progress and development.

Specification

This defines what you will need to do in order to get the project completed.

Planning

This is the process you will use to decide who will do what and how it will be done. You might find it helpful to use the '5 Cs' of decision-making.

1. Consider – what is the nature of the project, and what information do you need? (Identify objectives.)

2. Consult – as this is a project about consultation, it is crucial that people feel involved from the outset so that you are not seen to be paying lip service, or the project will be doomed from the start.

3. Crunch – take decisions and write down the action plan. It is better to make a poor decision than no decision which keeps others in limbo.

4. Communicate – ensure that you provide briefings, both verbal and backed up in writing in formats appropriate to your audience, so that everyone is engaged early on.

5. Check – that the briefings have been carried out, monitor effectiveness through spot checks, and take any remedial action.

Traditional project management methods of recording planning of actions include Gantt charts or PERT (Programme Evaluation and Review Technique) diagrams. There are also software programs such as Microsoft Project and MindGenius (which not only generates a project plan but also helps you to think through the issues first).

Alternatively, you could use a whiteboard and pen, or 'sticky notes' along a wall, to decide what steps need to happen and in what order to achieve your objectives.

If you want to know more about project management tools, the authors suggest you take a course in project management or read one of the excellent books on the subject (for example, *The Project Management Pocketbook* by Keith Posner and Mike Applegarth).

Communication
Other key considerations are: Work out how the project manager and their team will communicate with each other so that you can keep everyone 'in the loop'. How will the organisation know how you are getting on?

Timescale
How long will the whole project take? Build in milestones (critical deadlines) or smaller achievements within the project.

Resources
What resources will you need (cost, people, equipment and other resources) in order to complete the project?

Quality
What standard do you want project participants to aspire to? What should be the desired quality of the end result?

Implementation
This is the stage where you are now putting the plan into action, as closely as possible in line with your original objectives. Inevitably, things go wrong – so, to allow for this possibility, build in a contingency plan as you go along, as per Table 8.4.

Table 8.4 Control point identification chart

Control element	What can go wrong?	How and when will I know?	What will I do about it?
Quality			
Cost			
Time			

Whilst you are implementing the plan, don't forget that people may be struggling and need support and/or the relevant development. The team needs to feel that they are genuinely participating staff and service users. Ensure that they understand the nature of the change process and feel part of decision-making processes. For any new venture to succeed there is an element of RISK:

- Relationships within the team
- Information shared in the team
- Support from the project manager
- Kindness to listen to others, even though you are busy and don't fancy doing it!

Ensure that each team member gets time to feed back their progress, one-to-one for small stuff and at a team meeting for strategic issues.

Team theory

It has been said that all new groups go through a process of adaptation, of the individual to the group and the group to the individual, as part of their natural development. It may be helpful to recognise the following stages in order to help the group become a team:

- Forming – the group gets together and has a common aim.
- Storming – a short time later, aims and objectives are questioned and there is some internal conflict.
- Norming – as a result of the conflict, guidelines are established, so that there is an accepted way of working.
- Performing – the group accepts and adheres to the guidelines and works effectively towards the aim.

Evaluation

It is important to review the progress of the project at regular intervals and note what went well and what lessons have been learned for the future. Once the project is completed, you can also set up dates for reviewing the outcomes in the future, e.g. the policy review.

McKinsey's 7S model (cited in Posner and Applegarth 1998, p.91) can be used as a planning tool or as a review tool to look at the impact of the project and associated change to an organisation:

- Strategy – with the new service user consultation strategy, do we have congruence with our vision and business plan? If not, what needs to be amended?

- Systems – how will we ensure that systems are put in place and monitored to note the effectiveness of the new strategy?
- Staff – are they all familiar with the project, and accepting of it?
- Skills – are there outstanding training needs?
- Style – how well are we communicating now? Are there fewer misunderstandings?
- Shared values – do we now demonstrate that we uphold the ethos of valuing service user consultation and participation?
- Structure – are our reporting lines effective and efficient? Can we avoid needless bureaucracy?

SUMMARY

This chapter has in essence shown you what to do and how to plan and execute a consultation and involvement project. By using the models above and the following, final workbook section, you should have enough pointers to help you devise your own service user involvement strategy.

Workbook

This section enables you and your team or organisation to clarify how you are going to conduct the development of your strategy.

The following questions will help you work towards a comprehensive strategy for service user involvement, including policy, procedures and methods.

The questions may be answered individually, or used for the basis of a team discussion at any level of an organisation. You might like to write up your plans as a big chart and/or copy it to everyone (including the service users!) so that they know what is going on and when.

- What do you want to achieve? (Write this down so it is unambiguous and agreed!)
- What exactly needs to be done?
- How will it be done?

Personnel and task allocation:

Assign a participation/consultation officer, a member of staff who is enthusiastic about the concept of service user involvement, to oversee the development of a strategy, and coordinate service user involvement activities in general. Recognise that it could be a paid post, a secondment or, more usually, responsibility 'in name only', and give this role the responsibility and authority it needs and, ideally, a budget.

- Who will be the project team?
- Who will do what within the team?
- How long will this take?
- Build in milestones for progress review purposes and the satisfaction of getting somewhere!
- How often will they meet?
- How will decisions be made?
- What resources do you need?
- What is your budget?
- Where will you get the resources?
- How, what and when will you communicate to the rest of the organisation?
- How will you judge the quality of the work you are doing?
- What are the possible problems faced by the project?
- How will you deal with them if they occur?

The following may be useful goals:

- a policy document (we have provided a draft framework in previous chapters)
- a menu of ways in which service users can be consulted
- timescales for implementation and review
- a menu of activities that service users can engage in, e.g. recruiting staff
- management clarity about the degree to which service users will be involved, and the degree of influence their views will have
- deciding and agreeing on any expenditure or resources.

Appendix A – Questionnaire for providers

1. Would you be interested in attending training on   Yes/No
   user consultation methods?

2. If so, where would be a convenient geographical
   area for you to attend?

3. Do you work with any of the
   hard-to-reach/under-represented people below:
   (a) young people   Yes/No
   (b) people who have committed offences   Yes/No
   (c) people who are or have been homeless   Yes/No
   (d) women escaping domestic violence   Yes/No
   (e) people who have addiction issues   Yes/No
   (f) black and minority ethnic (BME) groups   Yes/No
   (g) people with complex needs   Yes/No

4. Are there people in your organisation whom you   Yes/No
   would rather we contact directly, who work with
   these groups?
   Please give contact name(s) and numbers(s):

5. Do you currently have any service user groups that   Yes/No
   meet?
   If so, please give details, so that we can add them to
   the directory.

6. How do you consult with service users currently, if at all?

   (NB this is not an exercise in guilt-making, but about finding ways of making it easier!)

   (a) at a personal level:

   (b) at the service level:

   (c) at the strategic level:

7. What barriers do you find get in the way of having a service user consultation strategy for strategic decision-making?

(a) do not know how to	Yes/No
(b) service users would need advocacy help	Yes/No
(c) no time to write a strategy	Yes/No
(d) worried about having service users at a strategic level	Yes/No
(e) hard to set aside time	Yes/No
(f) other.	Yes/No

8. How could we best communicate with your service users for this project?

a) staff distribution of information, e.g. posters/letters	Yes/No
b) website	Yes/No
c) arranging visits with them as individuals and/or groups within a service that they use.	Yes/No

Appendix B – Values statement

Values

Group members are committed to the belief that all people using supported housing services have the right to choose to be consulted about the services they are receiving now, and in the future, and about their preferred methods of effective consultation.

The group believes that involving current and ex-service users in planning for the future will improve the quality and effectiveness of those services.

Group members value diversity of membership in order to produce a wide range of opinions and achieve a greater level of creativity in finding effective consultation strategies.

Aims

- to develop effective and inclusive user consultation methods
- to present complex issues in as simple a way as possible, avoid jargon and provide a user-friendly environment for discussions
- to try to be honest about what can and cannot be changed or influenced outside the group
- to endeavour to research and build on established good or interesting practice.

Mechanism/method

- The project will trial and review various consultation methods for involving service users in strategic planning and actively seek advice and feedback from the good practice group.
- ALL project participants, steering and good practice group members will actively encourage and value the input of those using services and will take account of their views.

- Steering group and good practice group and reference group members will offer training and coaching to service users wishing to be part of the project if requested.
- All participants will genuinely share their power and ownership, communicate honestly and be respectful of individual needs.

Appendix C – Calculating the cost of client consultation

We have devised a 'Calculating the cost' checklist to help commissioners and providers plan and cost their client consultation strategy. You can adapt it for one-off exercises, a series of meetings, etc. It is by no means exhaustive but gives a clear structure to start to calculate the cost of client involvement.

	£ per hour, etc.	Total
Professionals		
Preparation for meetings		
Board discussion time		
Managers' time		
Staff teams' time		
Inter-agency meetings		
Professionals and clients		
Communications with clients		
Preparation/training of clients		

Continued on next page

Calculating the cost (cont.)	£ per hour, etc.	Total
Designing posters, questionnaires		
Holding workshops		
Holding open days		
Attending open days		
Attending training/development opportunities		
Defining strategy		
Consultation methods: • primary – meetings/questionnaires • secondary – drama, creative writing		
Clients seeking other clients' views		
Professionals and clients (cont)		
Monitoring and review		
Practical costs		
Room hire		
Food refreshments		
Crèche/childcare		
Transport		
Payment/reward/vouchers		

References

Arnstein, S.R. (1969) 'A ladder of citizen participation.' *Journal of the American Planning Association 35*, 4, 216–224.

Barnes, M. and Wistow, G. (1997) 'Understanding User Involvement.' In A.J. Pithouse and H. Williamson (eds) *Engaging the User in Welfare Services*. Nuffield Institute, Birmingham: Venture Press.

Begum, N. and Gillespie-Sells, K. (1994) *Towards Managing User-led Services*. London: The Race Equality Foundation.

Bewley, C. and Glendinning, C. (1994) *Involving Disabled people in Community Care Planning*. London: Joseph Rowntree Foundation.

Brafield, H. (2000) 'MBA's for Charity Managers: Are Charities Becoming More like Businesses? A Study of Four Not for Profit Agencies.' MBA Thesis. London: Imperial College, University of London

Brafield, H. (2003a) *Consulting with Hard to Reach Users of Housing Related Support Service at the Strategic Level for 'Supporting People'*. Southampton: ROCC.

Brafield, H. (2003b) *Guidance for Commissioners (for Consulting with Hard to Reach Users of Housing Related Support Service at the Strategic Level for 'Supporting People')*. Southampton: ROCC.

Cole, I., Hickman, P., Millward, L. and Reid, B. (1999) *Developing Good Practice in Tenant Participation – Housing*. London: Department of Transport and Regions.

Community Care Needs Assessment Project (CCNAP) (2001) '"Asking the Experts": A Guide to Involving People in Shaping Health and Social Care Services.' Grimsby: CCNAP. Available at www.ccnap.org.uk/layout.htm (accessed 6 November 2007).

Cornwall County Council Drug and Alcohol Team (2005) 'Key Theme 2 – Drugs and Alcohol.' Truro: Cornwall County Council Drug and Alcohol Team. Available at www.cornwall.gov.uk/index.cfm?articleid=10076 (accessed 6 November 2007).

Cummings, B., Dickson, A., Jackson, A.A., Jones, N., Laing, I. and Rosengard, A. (2000) *Young Homeless People Speaking for Themselves*. Edinburgh: Scottish Youth Housing Network.

Department of Skills and Education (DfES) (2003) *Every Child Matters*. London: The Stationery Office.

Department of Transport, Local Government and Regions (DTLR) (2002) *Reflecting the Needs and Concerns of Black and Minority Ethnic Communities in Supporting People.* London: DTLR.

Eckersley, T. (n.d.) 'My experience of service user involvement.' Unpublished document.

Eckersley, T. (n.d.) 'New York Housing – New England Corporate.' Unpublished document.

Firth, M. and Kerfoot, M. (1997) *Voices in Partnership – Involving Users and Carers in Commissioning and Delivering Mental Health Services.* London: The Health Advisory Service, The Stationery Office.

Groundswell UK (1997) *Toolkit for Change.* London: Groundswell.

Hackney Supporting People Team (2003) *London Borough of Hackney Strategy for User Involvement (Draft 2).* Unpublished document.

Hampshire County Council (2005) *The Hampshire Supporting People Strategy 2005–2010 Draft for Consultation.* Winchester: Hampshire County Council.

Hope, P. and Hargreaves, S. (1997) *User Involvement Principles and Practice for Users in the Design and Delivery of Public Services, a Framework.* London: Joseph Rowntree Foundation.

Housing Corporation (2002) *Implementing Best Value in Housing and Tenant Participation Compacts – the first year, Housing Research Summary.* London: Department of Local Government Regions.

Housing Corporation (2005) *The Regulatory Code and Guidance.* Available at www.housingcorp.gov.uk/upload/pdf/RegulatoryCode.pdf (accessed 6 November 2007).

Jones, R. (1995) 'Co-opting carers and users.' *Directors of Adult Social Services (ADSS) News,* April, 18–19.

Keeble, M. (2000) *Just Do It! A Directory of Examples of User Involvement in Supported Housing.* London: The Housing Corporation.

Lindow, V. (1999) *Evaluation of the National User Involvement Project, Social Care Research.* London: Joseph Rowntree Foundation. Available at http://www.jrf.org.uk/knowledge/findings/socialcare/ scr129.asp (accessed 5 November 2007).

Maslow, A.H. (1943) 'A Theory of Human Motivation.' *Psychological Review 50,* 370–96.

Office of the Deputy Prime Minister (ODPM) (2003) *Supporting People: A Guide to User Involvement for Organisations Providing Housing Related Support Services.* London: ODPM.

Office of the Deputy Prime Minister (ODPM) (2006) *Planning for Gypsy and Traveller Sites. ODPM Circular.* London: ODPM.

Posner, K. and Applegarth, M. (1998) *The Project Management Pocketbook.* Alresford: Alresford Press Ltd.

Race and Housing Inquiry Panel (2002) *Race Equality Code of Practice for Housing Associations.* Available at www.housing.org.uk/Uploads/File/Policy%20 briefings/race_codesofpractice.pdf (accessed 6 November 2007).

Robson, P., Begum, N. and Locke, M. (2003) *Increasing User Involvement in Voluntary Organisations.* London: Joseph Rowntree Foundation. Available at www.jrf.org.uk/knowledge/findings/ socialcare/723.asp (accessed 5 November 2007)

Robson, P., Locke, M. and Dawson, J. (1997) *User Involvement in the Control of Voluntary Organisations. Social Care Research 93.* Bristol: Policy Press in association with the Joseph Rowntree Foundation. Available at www.jrf.org.uk/knowledge/findings/socialcare/SC93.asp (accessed 4 November 2007).

Ross, K. (1995) 'Speaking in tongues: Involving users in day care services.' *British Journal of Social Work 25,* 791–804.

Southampton City Council (2002) *Race Equality Scheme 2002–2005.* Southampton: Southampton City Council.

Southampton City Council (2006) *Comprehensive Equality Policy.* Southampton: Southampton County Council.

Velasco, I. (2001) *Service User Participation. Concepts, Trends and Practices.* Edinburgh: Scottish Council for Single Homeless.

Ward, L. (1997) *Seen and Heard: Involving Disabled Children and Young People in Research and Development Projects.* London: Joseph Rowntree Foundation.

Watson, L., Tarpey, M., Alexander, K. and Humphreys, C. (2003) *Supporting People Real Change? Planning Housing and Support for Marginal Groups.* London: Joseph Rowntree Foundation.

Useful websites

www.advanceuk.org
Website of Advance. 'Advance is a charitable organisation providing housing, support and employment services to meet the needs of people in the community who have either a learning disability or a mental health problem... Advance does this as a registered housing association, a national provider of support services, and an accredited provider of employment services.'

alphauk.org
Website for the Alpha Course. 'Alpha is an opportunity for anyone to explore the Christian faith in a relaxed setting over ten thought-provoking weekly sessions, with a day or weekend away.'

www.amp.uk.net
'The voice of young people in Tower Hamlets.'

www.atlantichousing.co.uk
Website of Atlantic Housing Ltd. 'Atlantic Housing is the largest provider of social housing in Eastleigh. It manages and maintains affordable homes for rent or purchase and provides high quality housing services for its residents... As part of the First Wessex Housing Group, Atlantic Housing aims to be an outstanding landlord and service provider.'

www.bathnes.gov.uk/bathnes
Website of Bath and North East Somerset Council.

www.businessballs.com
Website offering resources for career training and development: 'inspirational, innovative ideas, materials, exercises, tools, templates – free and fun'.

www.ccnap.org.uk
Website of the Community Care Needs Assessment Project.

www.communities.gov.uk
Previously the Office of the Deputy Prime Minister.

www.connexions-southcentral.org

Website offering information and advice about the Connexions service in the South of England.

www.cornwall.gov.uk/index.cmf?articleid=36128

Website about the Cornwall and Isles of Scilly Drug and Alcohol Action Team.

www.drugs.gov.uk

This website provides drugs professionals with the latest news and guidance from government about the Drugs Strategy.

www.ficm.org

The website of Freedom in Christ Ministries.

www.groundswell.org.uk

Website about Groundswell. 'Groundswell is the leading user involvement and self-help organisation working in the field of homelessness in the UK. We believe homeless people are not the problem they must be part of the solution... Our directory enables homeless people's self-help and service user groups to contact and learn from each other, and be involved in creating practical solutions to their problems.'

www3.hants.gov.uk/supporting-people/sp-about-us/ sp-strategy.htm#5-

Hampshire County Council page indexing Supporting People Strategy Information.

www.jrf.org.uk

Website of the Joseph Rowntree Foundation. 'We are one of the largest social policy research and development charities in the UK, spending about £10 million a year on a research and development programme that seeks to better understand the causes of social difficulties and explore ways of overcoming them.'

www.spinnakergroup.co.uk/Medina

Website of the Medina Housing Association. 'Medina operates on the Isle of Wight and aims to provide excellent housing services, support and assistance to local households.

We are a community-focused association, aiming to deliver locally agreed services in line with our Neighbourhood Strategy. To this end, we are committed to working closely with our tenants, local residents and other key partners.'

www.refuge.org.uk

Website for the charity that provides 'a network of safe houses offering emergency accommodation for women and children when they are most in need.'

www.rocc.org.uk

Website for the charity ROCC (originally the Resettlement of Offenders Coordinating Committee), which was established in 1975 as an integral part of Hampshire Probation Service. The breadth of ROCC's work extended rapidly to include work with housing organisations providing for a wide range of client groups.

'The consultancy service has developed to meet the needs of service providers facing ever changing pressures in the social care environment, and all trainers and consultants are independent yet carry the values of ROCC to enable services to develop their professional skills and portfolios... In 2007, ROCC has a current membership in excess of 110 organisations and this continues to grow as ROCC further develops its information and advice, training and consultancy services to meet the needs of its many and varied stakeholders.'

www.surestart.gov.uk
Website of Sure Start, the government programme to 'deliver the best start in life for every child. We bring together, early education, childcare, health and family support.'

www.ccnap.org.uk/Guide/part1.htm
Swindon People First is a user-run self-advocacy group run by and for adults with learning difficulties.

www.ukyouth.org
Website for UK Youth, 'the leading national youth work charity supporting over 750,000 young people, helping them to raise their aspirations, realise their potential and have their achievements recognised via non-formal, accredited education programmes and activities.'

www.wesleyowen.com
Website for the 'new look Premier Christian Music website!'

www.smartchange.org
Website offering a way for companies and charities to get together. 'Smartchange for companies is a self-service employee giving solution.'

www.womensaid.org.uk
Website for the charity Women's Aid. 'Women's Aid is the national domestic violence charity that helps over 320,000 women and children every year.'

www.ymca.net/about/cont/history.htm
Website offering information about the history of the Young Men's Christian Association (YMCA).

www.ymca.org.uk
Website for YMCA England. 'We represent over 140 YMCAs supporting young people at every stage of their lives. From providing housing, training and community health and fitness facilities to supporting young people and their families, YMCAs in over 250 communities in England encourage, support and challenge young people to become all that they can.'

Subject Index

Author Index